Okay, I will admit Karen James ... Danielle and Shannon. Well, s ... know what an excellent book is. *On Purpose* is important because we all need to find the path to what matters in life. Reading is learning and learning is the path. We all need to get on one. Karen did...

— **Bob Gaudio, songwriter, producer, founding member of The Four Seasons, inspiration for the Jersey Boys**

On Purpose provides a simple formula to transcend your organisation's purpose into action and literally get everyone on-purpose. Karen's methods and leadership are exemplary, as experienced over the six years we have worked together. She is infectious and brings real purpose to any endeavour, including now her book.

— **Symon Brewis-Weston, CEO Sovereign Insurance (wholly owned by Commonwealth Bank), one of five business leaders to be awarded the Winner United Nations 2015 Women's Empowerment Principles Chief Executive leadership award**

Karen is one of the most purpose-driven people I have ever met. She operates with a strong sense of ethics and humanity. The philosophy and the framework behind *On Purpose* is great advice for anyone who wants to transform themselves and their organisation.

— **Janet Holmes à Court AC**

Today's world needs this book—delivered with wit, humour and cut through New York style, Karen's decade of experience in life and business is bottled up in a fable, a manifesto and a practical framework that will get you and your organisation on-purpose. The complex made simple. I love it and look forward to joining Karen to create a movement to mobilise on-purpose leaders.

—Ronni Kahn, CEO and Founder of OzHarvest, the first perishable food rescue organisation in Australia, now in its 10th year. Winner of Veuve Clicquot Initiative for Economic Development 2012, Ernst & Young Social Entrepreneur of the Year 2012, and Australian Local Hero of the Year 2010.

On Purpose is a book which simplifies Karen's deep understanding of how to make things happen in the business world into a framework for every person and organisation. Karen's ability to take an idea and turn it into reality is first class—and I know that firsthand from my participation in the Commonwealth Bank's Women in Focus program. For more than a quarter of a century through a journey of ups and downs that the faint-hearted would have given in, Karen's track record is *On Purpose*'s testimony. Getting to the how is as important as the why—*On Purpose* brings the two together in a formula that I look forward to promoting.

—Naomi Simson, Founding Director RedBalloon

on
PURPOSE

Why great leaders
start with the
PLOT

Karen James

WILEY

First published in 2015 by John Wiley & Sons Australia, Ltd
42 McDougall St, Milton Qld 4064
Office also in Melbourne

Typeset in 11/14 pt ITC Garamond Std by Aptara, India

© KBSN Pty Ltd 2015

The moral rights of the author have been asserted

National Library of Australia Cataloguing-in-Publication data:

Creator:	James, Karen, author.
Title:	On Purpose : Why great leaders start with the PLOT / Karen James.
ISBN:	9780730322467 (pbk.)
	9780730322474 (ebook)
Notes:	Includes index.
Subjects:	Business — Decision making.
	Business planning.
	Industrial management.
	Success in business.
Dewey Number:	658.406

All internal images and illustrations © KBSN Pty Ltd. Illustrations in Part I and III created by New Way Solutions, Argentina, and KBSN Pty Ltd.

Cover design by Wiley

Cover image: © Eivaisla/iStockphoto.com

Author photograph by Franki Pollick Photography

Printed in Singapore by C.O.S. Printers Pte Ltd

10 9 8 7 6 5 4 3 2 1

Disclaimer
The material in this publication is of the nature of general comment only, and does not represent professional advice. It is not intended to provide specific guidance for particular circumstances and it should not be relied on as the basis for any decision to take action or not take action on any matter which it covers. Readers should obtain professional advice where appropriate before making any such decision. To the maximum extent permitted by law, the author and publisher disclaim all responsibility and liability to any person, arising directly or indirectly from any person taking or not taking action based on the information in this publication.

To my daughters, Ashley and Madison
In memory of my mother—Kath, Mom, Gran

Live Life ON Purpose.

 Karen James

CONTENTS

FOREWORD

I loved this book and read it in one sitting, give or take a few tea and coffee breaks. Karen James has written about business in a fresh and beguiling way and it is understood from the beginning that she loves both business and education as I do. She just wants them to be better and her manifesto offers advice about how we might change.

These are not changes that require regulation by government but changes in how we play the game and take personal responsibility for change. She reminds us that values statements hanging on the company walls or coming up on the screen matter not a toss if people do not live them.

On Purpose is a cleverly constructed book, as we might expect from its engineer author. Each section can stand alone or be connected—a sublime literary and engineering feat.

The Fable evoked powerful memories for me as I reflected on my first classroom experience. Planning a career as a secondary school teacher I was surprised to be assigned to a primary school for my first practice teaching my postgraduate year. My supervisor considered that exposure and early practice with 8–12 year olds offered the best experience for a teaching career. He was right.

More than five decades later I work in different classrooms and boardrooms but how I loved being thrown back into Ms Molloy's classroom in Glen Fark County with a group of 8-year-olds whose first project of the year is to build a bank.

They go back to basics as they ask: What does a bank do? What is its purpose? Does it have values? Would we want to work there?

Ms Molloy suggests the children include their parents in the project and the outcomes are surprising but you need to read that for yourself.

On Purpose is a contemporary cautionary ethical tale, a fable we can all understand. It reminds us we should never underestimate the capacity of 8-year-olds to manage complexity with purpose, ethics and humanity, all the big words they were asked to consider as they followed the PLOT methodology. It was sad to leave Ms Molloy's classroom. It was an exciting learning place.

In the Manifesto our author writes of her central thesis that there must be a meaningful purpose at the core of our lives and our organisations. We need to keep our heads and hearts connected in order to live purpose-filled lives.

It is hard to disagree but for many of us we need to know how to achieve that.

The PLOT framework — Purpose, Leadership, Operations and Technology — is offered as a methodology to facilitate discussion, raise questions, challenge, gauge and monitor attainment of an on-purpose organisation.

This book could become the new black for business.

How could you not aspire to be on-purpose personally or professionally?

Wendy McCarthy AO
Educator, Mentor, Non-executive Director

ABOUT THE AUTHOR

Fast-talking, funny and pulling no punches, Karen James is a Jersey girl turned social entrepreneur who has risen through the ranks of the global corporate world while honouring her most important role in life as a proud single mother and humanitarian. From building with her team a 10 000-strong community of women within a leading bank, to integrating not-for-profit leadership lessons into corporate boardrooms and growing a company from a turnover of $9 million to a turnover of $100 million, Karen is a fixer and a doer who matches head with heart — and makes it everyone's business to do the same.

In her debut book, Karen applies the same pragmatic logic to timeless questions around creating purpose and building an organisation with humanity at its heart.

Her company, BEact Pty Ltd, helps others to embed this same logic into their own lives and organisations to create a truly sustainable world that we can all benefit from.

ACKNOWLEDGEMENTS

To my readers, thank you for taking the time and energy to read *On Purpose*. Without you the book has no purpose.

To my family and framily (friends who are family)—without you I would not be who I am today and I would not know how on earth anything would be possible. You are everything to me.

To my team who has been pivotal in this book, who believed in me and the idea, and who I look forward to working with as our journey continues.

To the community of women who have united to help each other—you believed in me, you let me dance like Ellen, and you lit the flame for this book.

To the people I have worked with, and for, over many years and countries—thank you for trusting and believing in me and my ideas.

To my creative Argentinian illustrators for bringing the characters of the fable to life.

To Wiley for giving me the opportunity to publish this book and bring it to life.

To the gift from above. I know my hand is not on my steering wheel and I am humbled to be given the life I have. Thank you for putting PLOT in my heart and for directing me to turn right (you will understand this after you read *On Purpose*).

INTRODUCTION

A business book with a fable; why read it?

'Interesting', you may think (or not!)—'what's that all about?'. Let me introduce you to *On Purpose*, a book of three parts: The Fable (Back to School); the Manifesto; and PLOT, the business book.

Sometimes going back and seeing things the way we did when we were children helps us to clarify what's really important and why. The fable takes you on the journey of a teacher setting her Grade 3 students the assignment of building a bank. Along the way a diverse group of eight-year-olds learn important lessons about ethics and humanity and how these values need to be woven into the organisations of our future.

The second part of the book is the bridge between the fictitious and the future. Aptly titled, the Manifesto is a declaration of intentions. It unpacks the intentions of *On Purpose* and its fable in preparation for practical application in your business, and potentially your life—bringing intentions to the front of the classroom.

The third part of the book is the practical application—showing how great businesses PLOT their success by linking **P**urpose, **L**eadership, **O**perations and **T**echnology. At the end of this book you will understand the importance of making purpose the driver of your organisation, and be able to practically monitor your progress through the purpose-led PLOT Framework.

On Purpose is a book to act on.

The Fable (Back to School)

Many years ago I realised that I was a storyteller—at home, at work, at play. At work it seemed that there were many stories: it was the story of the customer, the story of the employee, the story of the vision, the story of success that always hit the mark much faster than the documents, PowerPoint presentations and reports. These stories connected us all through our humanity. So it seemed natural to begin with a fable to interpret the context of the book through the eyes of a child, and through the subtle lessons of life that are so readily seen when we are young.

My life has been shaped by my 'teachers': my school teachers; my mother; my grandmother Bebe; my great-aunts; my cousins; and my 'framily' (friends who have become family). We need teachers. Without teachers we believe the rhetoric, and when we believe the rhetoric we start behaving as though it is the truth.

There is something very humbling about being a student, being open to learning and being open to change—and opportunity often lies in the shadow of change. The fable introduces the purpose-led PLOT Framework through innocence, creativity, opportunity, a dash of humour and connection. I hope you connect with one or more of the characters. It is connection with the characters of our world that binds us and creates the magic.

I don't want to spoil the fable so I shall leave you to read on. Look for the subtle leadership lessons—they are fast and furious.

Manifesto

Engineers are taught early on the importance of the simple truss when building bridges—that beautiful structural frame based on the geometric strength of the triangle. This book's bridge, the Manifesto, binds (or trusses) the fable to the world of business by outlining the importance of intentions. It is a passage out of the fable and into the business book, simplifying and strengthening the message of the importance of being and acting on-purpose in today's changing world.

PLOT

The third part of the book, PLOT, provides a framework for organisational and business application of **P**urpose, **L**eadership, **O**perations and **T**echnology and, most importantly, explains how to instil and ingrain these into our lives — at home and at work. Our purpose (the thing that really matters) and meaning (the reason it matters to us) are foundational, but without action it is just a story. We need to know *how* to do this. Practically. *On purpose.* I don't mean the idiom that gets thrown at you when you are a child. I'm talking about compelling purposes you live and work by, and the ability to turn those intentions into actions.

The Action chapter introduces three tools to bring it all to life. The PLOT Framework acts as a gauge to track how your purpose and leadership are integrated into your operations and technology. The customisable mobile app brings the message alive by sharing purpose, leadership, what you are doing and how you are doing things — creating a storyboard that celebrates your success, chronicles your journey and connects everyone along the way. The presentation templates (PowerPoint and Prezi) are included in the event that you are a bit like me and enjoy the story but not the documentation.

* * *

Linking and threading purpose seamlessly through leadership, operations and technology is hard work and is a relentless pursuit. Pull one thread out and you start to unravel the possibility of greatness and success. This is the key point of the book and the PLOT Framework — all four matter in our unpredictable, digitised future.

My hope for you is that you enjoy and are transformed by this book, one page at a time.

PART I

The Fable (Back to School)

W e've all been eight years old, innocent and wide-eyed. We've all been students willing and wanting to learn. And we've all had a teacher we loved.

This modern-day fable seeks to help us find—and stay true to—our purpose when we're charting off course.

Our fable is set in Glen Fark County, post GFC, in a world where reality TV takes precedence and the size of celebrities' derrières is at the front of too many people's minds.

Our all-seeing narrator takes us into Ms Molloy's classroom, where a class of students will soon begin work on one of their most challenging assignments yet: learning leadership lessons of a complex business world and staying true to these, no matter the circumstance.

It's an adult world—you'd think, at least—so the children seek a little help from one of the parents, Bob. Bob is a hard-working banker (and, as you will soon see, many of us have worked for, or with, a 'Bob').

I hope you enjoy the fable in all its irony, which may weave some morals and lessons through a little piece of your world. Some are stated, some are subtle and some are specific only for a few of us—unique for 'our' stories. A free-form Smartboard has been created in the back of the book for the note-takers like me (give me digital, but please let me keep my Moleskine notebook). With or without notes, it, as we say in New Jersey, may help you to get shit done.

Oh, just one more thing: every good fable features an animal and this one is no different. There's an elephant in the room. See if you can find it…

Meet the characters

Ms Molloy   Mrs Laforte   Mrs Doogan   Vikki   Steve

Bob   Bobby   Nicholas   Abby   Sally

Julia   Betsy   David & Johnny Hehman

The adults

Ms Molloy teaches Glen Fark County Elementary School's Grade 3 class, which is filled with wide-eyed eight-year-olds. She is a firm but fair teacher with a huge heart. Our narrator will introduce you to her shortly.

Mrs Laforte is the assistant principal, a career teacher committed to the betterment of children and society. She has a heart of gold and coaches the teachers regularly to be bold and creative.

Mrs Doogan is the wire-haired, affable principal, who knows she has to follow the rules although she would rather get back to basics and hug the children like she used to in the 1970s.

Vikki is Betsy's mum and works in the IT industry. She loves getting involved in the school and is committed to making sure her daughter Betsy has everything that a two-parent-family child has.

Steve works for Synergy Bank and looks after the school banking program. He knows the importance of good customer service but is often torn between customers and process.

Bob is a banker who works in New York City. He grew up in a working-class blue-collar town in New Jersey, and grafted his way to Wall Street. Bob is a family man, a businessman, and—well, you will learn more about him as you read on.

The students

Bobby is the son of Bob the banker. Bobby is not sure of himself and is sometimes nervous. He knows he wants to be more than the influences around him.

Nicholas is earnest and eager. He is very smart and has a sharp sense of bringing the team with him. Nicholas builds bridges between people even at the young age of eight.

Abby is quiet but profound. Most of the class knows she has the answers; they just need to give her the chance to be heard. Sally and Abby are good friends.

Sally has the nickname 'Swivel Neck' because she is always turning around in class and just cannot sit still. She is constantly observing but she is also a bit of a chatterbox. Sally has itchy feet, so they say.

Julia is a very smart high achiever. She should probably be advanced a year and put in a program for the gifted. Julia sometimes forgets to wait for her classmates to catch up.

Betsy is a natural sharer with an innate sense of empathy. She loves helping others and is very determined to do so.

David and Johnny Hehman are the twin sons of a controversial investment banker. They are relatively new to town and are often getting in trouble.

CHAPTER 1
BACK TO SCHOOL

> The purpose of life is a life of purpose.
>
> —*Robert Burns*

O nce upon a time, in a land filled with wi-fi, 24-hour news and too much fast food, our teacher Ms Molloy prepared for the school year ahead.

Ms Molloy knows she has a big year ahead of her—new students, an updated curriculum, a daily goal of 10 000 steps (always tracked on her wrist), and the usual aches and pains that come from dealing with a few high-maintenance parents and their long-suffering kids.

What Ms Molloy doesn't realise is that this year she will create a ripple effect that will change a family's life forever, for the better, and that countless others will benefit from her teachings.

Why? Because Ms Molloy lives her life on-purpose and she has a plan. Without a plan, purpose can be meaningless, and a purpose without meaning quickly loses its way.

Ms Molloy's purpose is to make a measured difference in the development of her students, particularly those from disadvantaged families. Her *how,* which helps her to act with her purpose in mind, is evident in the way she treats her students: with respect, equality and a firm eye on their future.

This is why Ms Molloy's teachings are not just about school but also about life—and, specifically for this assignment, about business.

I am the narrator, by the way, better known as the voice that appears as a thought bubble above people's heads. I am that guiding, nagging feeling we all get when our gut tickles away at our conscience. I jump forward or backward in time to hold a mirror up to the truth when the occasion requires.

But back to Ms Molloy. Every year Ms Molloy asks the kids in her class to build their own organisation. She loves the hands-on teaching experiences it gives. But this year she wants to take it further, to immerse the children as much as possible in their assignment, so that the lessons on business, humanity and life are abundantly clear and felt by all—through the *how*, or the *doing*, as Ms Molloy often calls it.

To kick-start these sessions and frame them in a little context, she plans to introduce what she calls New Big Words.

Each year Ms Molloy's New Big Words change to reflect the tide of trends and the shift in the global picture. Today she is at her desk at home with the fresh smell of autumn blowing through her window and a cup of tea sweating on the coaster.

She's doodling away in the big white sketchpad that she buys ten at a time from the local stationers and fills solely with words. Those clean paper surfaces always help the right words to flow forth, and her sketchpad moments give her great satisfaction.

This year, Ms Molloy has decided that her New Big Words are 'humane', 'humanity', 'ethical' and 'collaborate'. These four words are vigorously circled in her sketchpad, springing forth from the mind map that surrounds them. She's chosen these words to show her students how they can become courageous leaders who put humanity into the heart of smart business, with good outcomes resulting when grounded in the details of *doing*.

But on with the story. It opens at the start of a new school year at Glen Fark County Elementary, in a Grade 3 classroom where there are more *Frozen* lunchboxes and Minecraft drink bottles than one could even imagine.

Welcome to Ms Molloy

The playground at GFC Elementary School, New Jersey, is buzzing with the frenetic kind of excitement that goes nowhere and everywhere all at once.

It is the first day of the new school year, which means plenty of tears and heartache. 'And that's just the parents', Ms Molloy thinks to herself as she scrapes old adhesive off the classroom walls with her fingernail.

Ms Molloy is not your typical teacher (if there even is such a thing). She values teachings that are humane and ethical and thinks large scale: for the collaborative betterment of humanity. It might sound rather large and lofty, but Ms Molloy is nothing if not serious about her ability to teach others.

Her teaching tactics divide the parents and teachers around her. Some love her purpose-driven teaching style while others resent their child missing out on the participation prize they had earmarked for display.

Regardless, Ms Molloy knows she is here to create opportunities that empower her students to think independently. Ironically, it's what they did at the start of their lives, but fear and traditional education has a habit of intercepting this gift along the way.

The interception lives on, of course. Just look at how many adults are quick to agree to bad ideas during workplace powwows because they are frightened to speak their mind — or worse, because they don't know how to. 'If only "confrontation" wasn't such a bad word', Ms Molloy thinks, as she reaches for her phone.

As her wandering thumb starts dancing around her favourite social media sites, a strange ball of emptiness starts growing in her stomach. 'Why are you wasting your time with this?' she chides herself, turning her phone face down. Ms Molloy always asks *why*. This emerging global shift towards the *why* is not the reason she turns to the word so often. Not at all. Ms Molloy was taught the power of *why* by her down-to-earth mother and her training at university.

'The word "why" will always eventually lead you back to what is important', her favourite teacher, Geoff Jones, had explained, his shirt button undone in the days when hairy chests were all the rage. 'When confronted or at a crossroads, keep asking your future students and yourself *why* until there is no place to go, except the truth.'

Ms Molloy still believes in the power of those three letters — and she hears her students ask *why* enough times to know its effect. But she has realised that having the *why* without the *how* is like having only one side of a conversation. You need to be clear on your purpose, and know *how* you are going to bring it to life, for real change to take place.

Keep asking why, *until there's no place to go except the truth.*

To this day, whenever Ms Molloy asks her students *why*, she digs down to the heart of what is real. When she asks them *how* they are going to do the *why*... well, that's where the hard work starts. Ms Molloy knows these are big questions for young people, but by asking them to build these questions into their day-to-day lives now, the *why* and the *how* should become second nature to them in their adult years.

Ask an eight-year-old *why* and you never know what you might uncover.

Ms Molloy has already put her term teaching plan together. She has always been the kind of person who gets an endorphin rush from stocking up on materials for the year.

When the last corner of her teaching plan is stuck to the back of the door, Ms Molloy thinks back to last year's new organisation assignment. It had caused a stir when the children went home to tell their parents all about the New Big Words, in very solemn voices. She had sent the students home with oversized printouts of the New Big Words, hoping they would start to bring these values into their lives, even on a subconscious level. The printouts were plastered with gaudy glitter, which did nothing to win over the less conspiratorial parents, either.

This year Ms Molloy has decided the organisation will be a bank. Banks are topical and often in the news, so she is confident this will get her class thinking about the New Big Words, even if they are yet to be embraced by all the banks. Ethical leadership values are becoming more accepted as part of the curriculum, and are expected to take more of a centre stage in business. Ms Molloy's socially responsible New Big Words now had a place.

Not just a place. They would change lives. But we're jumping ahead of ourselves, because in this fable, as in life, opportunity often lies in the shadow of change.

Week one, day one

Purpose-setting

The bell is still a little while off and Ms Molloy has scheduled some time to sit and reflect. She believes that you must plan time to do what is important and you must honour this as you would any other appointment, or it won't happen. Nothing happens until it is scheduled.

She sits on her favourite padded chair in the classroom and carries out a quick ritual that she likes to perform before any meeting, but especially before meeting her students for the very first time: a recap of her purpose.

As it is for many, Ms Molloy's purpose has been borne out of frustration and knowing what she *did not* want to do. Knowing what you don't want is just as important as knowing what you do want. Her purpose comes from having dived into those things around her that frustrate her most deeply, knowing she could do them better, and then choosing the one that matters most to her.

Ms Molloy's years of frustration were at 'the system'. She saw too many students being disadvantaged by a lack of money, support or structure, and she knew how it felt. While she had not been brought up in poverty, her upbringing had skated close to it. There were days when they would only eat cereal for dinner and there were other days when dinners became more healthy affairs, depending on her mother's work. They would try to make this fun, calling their 'breakfast dinners' 'upside-down' days, but everyone around the table knew better.

Paying for an excursion was always a big deal, much as her mother tried to make out that it wasn't. Ms Molloy would stay at home and feign illness. She secretly hoped someone from school might phone up to see what was happening, but no-one ever did.

These days, Ms Molloy is quick to spot children acting in her younger mirror-image. She understands those who lack the brazen confidence that can come from a young life of privilege. This is why her purpose is to make a measured difference in the development of her students, particularly those from disadvantaged families. She believes we are all deeply connected and equal—even more so now that technology has built a net around us.

And so Ms Molloy prepares to meet the latest melting pot of complex and wonderful eight-years-young. Each is striving to be heard and accepted for who they are, before the world tries to change them too much.

The stampede

Ms Molloy walks out into the sunshine to survey the playground and the new school parents tightly holding their kindergarten child's hand. It always amazes her how quickly these children grow from barely toddlers into mostly confident little people.

Ms Molloy smiles the biggest smile she can manage as new students walk towards her one by one.

Once the rabble is settled in the classroom, the usual personalities are quick to present themselves. 'The leader who disregards everybody?' she thinks. 'Check. The hard worker who tries to please everyone but themselves? Check. The ones who try to get away with doing as little as possible for as long as possible, while having lots of fun in the process? Of course.' The labels are just a bit of fun, though. In reality she enjoys challenging her first impressions as the children mature over the year.

But there is one label that seems timeless: the considerate, thoughtful child who isn't driven by ego. The child who is wise beyond their years. They stand out for not needing to stand out, yet when they are required to lead with courage, they do so effortlessly — much to the surprise of the all-talking, all-cartwheeling peers around them.

These early school moments, wedged in between the first and second bells at the start of term, are always a beautiful thing to behold — beautiful and chaotic all at once. It always reminds Ms Molloy of her purpose. She will breathe humanity into this largely insecure and restless room of children who are approaching the tipping point where they forget their kindergarten selves in a desperate bid to find their way forward. This is the process Ms Molloy wants to undo. She wants this rabble to live their lives true to their calling, listening along the way with the courage to make it happen.

But today time simply passes in a blur of paperwork, new books and lost pencils. The final bell rings all too soon, as it often seems to when people are in the flow of being fully engaged and stimulated.

As the students file out of the room and head for home, Ms Molloy makes a cup of tea and sits at her desk with only the birds outside the window for company.

Her *how* inevitably bubbles to the surface, as is the way in quiet moments where she dedicates time to focus on this. 'I am going to lead with courage and make sure that I always act in the best interests of others—not what I want, not what the system wants, but what I know to be true and ethical and for the benefit of these children and their futures', she reminds herself. 'If I do this, I will always stay on-purpose.'

And with that, she packs up her bag, puts the last chair on top of the table for the cleaner, and heads home.

Week one, day three

The assignment

After settling her students in and reminding them where to get lunch, where the new toilets are—and stressing the importance of good hygiene—Ms Molloy decides the time is right to introduce her first assignment, the bank-building exercise.

'Girls and boys', Ms Molloy announces to the class of fidgety eight-year-olds, some of whom she is convinced have worms. 'We are going to build a business this term, and it is going to be a bank.'

She knows the children had expected to do their times tables or open their reading books, so this announcement has come as a complete surprise. Mere moments later, spit bombs explode out of the mouths of the Hehman brothers, a pair of frankly arrogant twins who like to rebel. The idea of building a successful organisation had clearly brought out their love of saliva-soaked aviation and their aversion to regulation.

So Ms Molloy does what she always does when the class starts to get to fever pitch: she asks *why*.

'Why are you all so restless this morning?' she asks.

'Because we are so excited!' replies Nicholas, an earnest student who is already bored with the level of mathematics for his age group.

'We want to make lots of money to buy stuff!' he says. 'And I've never built a business before, except when I helped my sister with her lemonade stand.

'Thank you Nicholas', says Ms Molloy. 'It is important to understand the value of money, and I hope that we can learn about its power and potential together as a class.

'Now, let's start on the New Big Words', she says, as she brings out this year's glittery, oversized sheets of paper to start the assignment.

New Big Words

The glitter makes a trail over her desk and gets under her fingernails as she holds up one of the pieces of cardboard she has painstakingly replicated 25 times in the past few days so that each child could bring one home.

'Okay everyone', she says. 'Can we read these New Big Words together on the count of three?'

'One, two, th—'

'It never works, the kids always jump the gun at two', Ms Molloy reminds herself, not sure why she insists on counting the students in.

'Our New—Big—Words...', they read aloud.

humane *(adjective)*: tender, compassionate and sympathetic

humanity *(noun)*: the quality of being humane and kind

ethical *(adjective)*: relating to right and wrong behaviour

collaborate *(verb)*: to work jointly on an activity or project

As Ms Molloy hands the cardboard out to each student, she tells the children they need to hang their sheet up somewhere special at home and 'be' like these words if they are going to really succeed in their organisation.

'Because a good organisation starts at home', she tells the children. 'We don't have different values for work and for home; we should bring the same values to work as well.'

Ms Molloy knows she shouldn't be too instructive here, but she can't help herself. She has a flashback to her first job, before she became a teacher, when her boss spoke about truth, honesty and integrity—right up until he was jailed for insider trading. Ms Molloy never did realise that her boss *did* have the right intentions, but fear made him fall short of his goals. He wished he had been more courageous as a leader and less of a charlatan.

* * *

The class is staring with wide eyes at the New Big Words, and wondering what these have to do with running a bank.

To set some context, Ms Molloy asks the students when they last behaved like the New Big Words. Arms soon extend far beyond the reach of their shoulder sockets, prompting Ms Molloy to choose Nicholas.

'I know all about these New Big Words because when my parents went to the bank last week, they came home and used these very same words!' he says.

Ms Molloy doesn't know that Nicholas's parents, who are starting their own business, recently had a fantastic experience with Synergy Bank, which is new to the area. The business banker actually came to their home to work through the bank's five lending criteria. Once the bankers understood the character of Nicholas's parents and they could apply this to a customer-centric framework, the transactions seemed to happen pretty seamlessly. Nicholas's parents felt understood and respected.

'My parents said that ever since the bank got a new manager who fixed their internet banking, looked at their mortgage, helped them start their business, and spoke to them kindly, they feel like the bank is actually on their side more.

'Is this an example of how these words work in business?' Nicholas asks fervently.

'Yes it is Nicholas!' says Ms Molloy, who could run up and hug Nicholas for getting this so quickly.

She hopes the other teachers were able to hear this lateral approach to teaching in action and wanders over to the window next to room 201 just in case. Every day Mr Aitkens writes an exhausting diatribe on the board for his Grade 2 class and asks the children to copy it into their exercise books. Even he doesn't seem to know why he does this. He works hard at it and is often stressed by his work, yet this hard work doesn't seem to get him or his students anywhere.

Ms Molloy is on a mission to help Mr Aitkens find his purpose and his *how*.

'So are we having fun, kids?' asks Ms Molloy, raising her voice a few octaves for the benefit of Mr Aitkens.

'YESS!!!!!' they roar, drowning out his monotone warbling through the walls.

Ms Molloy now turns on the Smartboard and begins by reminding the children what money is and why we need it. It's an easy task every year, because all the children know what money is: it is what they need to buy what they want.

Next Ms Molloy asks the class to look at the Smartboard and read out 'What is a bank?' Ms Molloy crafted these words the night before, staying up far too late as she often did when her mind went into overdrive right before bedtime.

'What is a bank?' the class reads out loud.

The bank looks after people's money for them and keeps it safe.

While they are looking after your money it grows — it gets a little bigger. This is called 'interest'.

The bank also gives money to people who need to buy things, like a house.

When the bank gives you money they lend it to you, meaning you have to pay it back and give back 'interest'. Nicholas and Julia read this statement twice as fast as the other students did, as they have done all day, before slowing down politely to fit in with the rest of class (which strikes Ms Molloy as a shame).

Turning back to the Smartboard before the class is tempted to start talking, Ms Molloy quickly writes down four Big Questions in big colourful letters. 'These are four Big Questions I want you to ask yourselves as you run your organisation', she explains. 'They will come up time and time again as we explore what it might be like to run a bank.'

The words are fairly adult in their approach, but Ms Molloy has faith in her students.

1 What is the *purpose* of the bank?

2 How will people at the bank need to *behave*?

3 What will the people at the bank need to *do*?

4 What will you need to do to make the bank *work*?

Dividing the groups

Before explaining the questions further, Ms Molloy divides the class into two groups and asks them to choose a leader — someone they think acts like the New Big Words.

'What are the New Big Words again?' asks Ms Molloy before the groups separate.

Excited, Betsy quickly raises her hand. 'Humane, humanity, ethical and collaborate', she exclaims.

Ms Molloy had noticed Betsy many times before she joined her class. The sweet girl always lends her well-worn Harry Potter books to others on the playground. Despite living in a relatively well-to-do area, there are still kids who struggle and can easily go unnoticed. Books are a luxury not all kids can afford, as Ms Molloy and the other teachers have come to understand over the years. It seems that Betsy has not been oblivious to it either.

'That's right', Ms Molloy says with a smile.

'Now, your job is to connect these words to the Big Questions and see how they can work together. You may refer to the definitions if necessary. This is how you build an organisation that is truly successful.'

Ms Molloy was surprised how much values can become blurred without the clarity of purpose-driven leadership in place. Even those companies that look successful on the outside can struggle internally when they don't match these values to meaningful purpose and live it every day through their actions.

Betsy is immediately chosen as the leader in her group, with no dispute. The children, in their huddle, all agree that she is so very kind because she often plays with students who are being ignored or picked on.

Betsy is quietly pleased—because, like all good leaders, she wants to make a positive difference in her bank, and also have everyone in the group enjoy the assignment. Not that Betsy would articulate it this way yet; it is largely instinctive to this eight-year-old with a big heart and a sharp mind.

The other group is also talking animatedly and, after much discussion, it is decided that Bobby will be the leader of this group. Everyone knows his dad is a banker and they reason that this will help them a lot. Bobby also has the biggest house and a pool with a creepy-crawly that operates all by itself. These things matter when you're eight years old.

With the team leaders now chosen, Ms Molloy calls for quiet. 'Now that we have our leaders, let's look at the Big Questions again', she says, flicking the Smartboard back to life.

1 What is the *purpose* of the bank?

2 How will people at the bank need to *behave*?

3 What will the people at the bank need to *do*?

4 What will you need to do to make the bank *work*?

'We will focus on one question each week, and we will do this only in class time', says Ms Molloy. 'I am also excited to announce that if you get any ideas from your classmates this will not be called "copying". It is called "collaborating", and it is one of our New Big Words.

'The world is changing, and sharing ideas just like children naturally do is now okay in business', Ms Molloy says as she points to the definition of 'collaborate'.

A wry smile comes across her face — this has been on her to-do list since last year. Ms Molloy fondly remembers when her university friend created a computer program using open-source code. Back in the 1980s it was deemed copying, so her friend failed the class, in spite of her protests. Oh the modern joys of collaboration!

'In school, creativity is just as important as literacy', Ms Molloy adds. 'Aren't we lucky, class?'

Betsy's team

After lunch, while Ms Molloy stands at the Smartboard going through the four questions once more, Betsy starts to think about her own parents and the bank.

It is easy for her to remember times her parents have described how the bank made them feel, but she can't think about a time they talked about what they were actually buying. It is as though the feeling that the bank gave them was the most important thing ...

When Betsy gets upset her mother always asks her what she is feeling. So this seems a good place to start when working out the purpose of their bank. Betsy asks the group what people might feel like when they use the bank — the good bits and the bad.

The group soon makes a list of all the 'feeling' words they've heard adults say: frustrated, happy, not fair, confused, thankful, stressed, grateful — plus some words they're not supposed to say. It is a very long list and they cannot believe how different some of the feelings are within their group.

There is a lot of frustration here, which makes them a little confused. When they think of other businesses, like the ice cream shop, they can think of only happy words. The group talks about this and thinks maybe it is because sometimes you have to give the money back to the bank—and no-one ever has to give back their ice cream once they've got it! They all agree they would rather run ice cream stalls.

Betsy thinks it best to check in with Ms Molloy at this point. Ms Molloy surveys this long list of 'feeling' words and does a silent high-five in her head. What a creative start to finding their bank's purpose!

She suggests that they now match this list of sometimes-frustrated 'feeling' words to the New Big Words, as this will help uncover the purpose a little more. And so the group starts to do this, using their intuition along the way. Every time they come to a frustrated word, they realise it could have been a much happier word if 'humane', 'humanity', 'ethical' or 'collaborate' had played a bigger role in the experience.

Bobby's group

Meanwhile, over in Bobby's group everyone decides that Bobby should speak to his dad first. He would know all the answers to these four Big Questions because he is a banker *and* he won the main prize at the school trivia night. He would just tell them their purpose and everyone would follow it.

Bobby thinks this is a sensible idea. He is quietly annoyed that the Hehman brothers are ignoring him and making up their own rules in the corner, but he knows Ms Molloy will get them in trouble eventually. And when you get in trouble with Ms Molloy it means you have really misbehaved. She is always fair, it seems—and as their teacher she is consistent with this, so you know what to expect.

Once the decision for Bobby to talk to his dad has been made, the children in his group decide to stop working on the assignment and just have some fun—at least until Ms Molloy notices!

Ms Molloy does indeed notice, and right before David Hehman loads up a spit ball to throw at Betsy's group she silences the group with that small, important word: *Why?*

The group stares back with the blank faces they usually reserve for video games, while David tucks the spit ball under his sleeve for safekeeping. He doesn't get why Ms Molloy would randomly say 'why' all the time; he thinks it is a bit weird, but the rest of the class seems to understand and answer the question honestly.

'Because we are going to speak to Bobby's dad and he will tell us how to run a bank because he's a banker ...?' stammers Nicholas.

Despite feeling pleased that Nicholas rose honestly to the challenge, Ms Molloy is not happy with this upward delegation and lack of responsibility.

To empower the group she says, 'I understand that Bobby's dad is a banker, thank you Nicholas'.

In truth, she knows it all too well. Last summer the school's assistant principal, Mrs Laforte, had requested Bobby's dad come in and help the school review a few ideas it had for raising funds and matching government grants. Bobby's dad was too busy and he let the school know that they should just go to the branch.

Ms Molloy turns her attention back to Bobby's group. 'Why don't you all collaborate as equals right now?' she says, looking at Nicholas, Bobby, the Hehman brothers and the rest of the group.

'I want to know everyone's suggestions — not just the banker's. There can be enormous power when we all lean in and allow everyone to have a say regardless of who they are', Ms Molloy adds, pleased that she managed to introduce this powerful pop culture reference to her Grade 3 class.

The joy is short-lived. An uncomfortable silence falls over the children. Ms Molloy reminds herself they are only eight years old. Then the bell rings and it is time to go home. Not a great start for Bobby's group.

Bobby's house

Bobby can't wait to tell his dad, Bob (Senior), that he is the leader of the group and he is going to build a bank! He gets off the school bus and runs up the driveway even though he knows his dad won't be home yet. Checking the mail, he unlocks the front door, remembering to leave the bills out for his parents on the kitchen table and he grabs himself a bowl of ice-cream before sitting in front of the TV.

As the cartoons play on, Bobby thinks about his first task—to answer Big Question 1. Bobby is very aware he hasn't got a clue how to answer it, but his dad will:

1 What is the *purpose* of the bank?

His dad works hard, which means they don't see each other much. There are annual holidays, and weekends at their beach house, but they are fleeting. Bobby's mother is an amazing woman who defies stereotypes. Her recently completed PhD in social policy lends itself to lively dinner-party conversation with Bob's work colleagues.

Bobby's mother makes his favourite dinner, meatballs with letter-shaped pasta, and Bobby can't wait to eat it so he can visit his dad in the study and tell him all about his day. He hopes his dad will be impressed.

Bob is in the study working on his laptop but when he hears the familiar light knock, he turns around to face Bobby with a big smile and tired eyes, ready to hear about his day.

'Dad, I am going to be just like you and I am going to run a bank! And we need to start by figuring out its purpose!' Bobby blurts out as he sits on his lap, wiggling his bony bottom into his dad's thighs with excitement.

'Well, I don't run a bank, I work for one', his dad replies with a chuckle and a wince as his thigh takes another bony wriggle.

'Yes you do, you totally run the bank! So, I need to know how to run a bank, starting with what its purpose is and then I will tell the group and we will do it.'

Bob laughs at his son's simplicity, then hops online and gives Bobby a rundown of his bank's:

- mission statement

- vision statement

- values and principles

- sustainability statement

- diversity statement

- key performance indicators (KPIs)—these things are needed so everyone can get paid a bonus, but only if they follow all the statements and values.

Bobby finds all of this a bit too much and can't quite figure out when to use the vision statement over the mission statement, let alone all the other statements and values.

He also cannot understand why there are only five values. He keeps thinking of all the things he has been taught since kindergarten (things like 'share everything', 'clean up your own mess', 'don't take things that aren't yours'), which all seem very relevant. But Bobby naturally assumed his dad, the best banker in the whole world, was right. So he stuck with the mission statement, even though he wasn't sure how to explain this back to the group just yet.

He also couldn't work out how he was going to measure everything they did, to see how well they worked or not. But having heard his dad talk so much about shareholders he decided they must be the people who judged everything—if only he knew who these important people were.

He asks his dad earnestly and Bob takes his glasses off to rub his eyes. 'A shareholder is someone who holds shares of stock in a company', he explains.

This makes no sense to Bobby so he presses on cautiously, not wanting to disappoint his dad. 'Why would anyone want to do that—and what are shares?'

Bob knew this was going to get messy so he tries his best to keep his answer simple. 'Shares are little pieces of the company and people buy shares and hold them so they can get something like interest.'

Bobby remembers Ms Molloy's paragraph on the wall about what the bank does, so with great excitement he shouts, 'I understand, Dad! Shareholders are a bit like the bank's customers, the ones who give and take money from the bank, only they're more important!'

His dad raises his eyebrows quizzically at Bobby and gives him a wry smile, before switching on the lamp to focus again on clearing his emails for the night. The next onslaught would come throughout the night from the bank's global offices and he knows if he doesn't get on top of his emails now he will pay for it tomorrow. It is like sweeping up leaves in the middle of a windstorm.

Jumping off his dad's lap and heading back down the corridor to do his homework, Bobby starts to wonder why he has never heard his dad talk about their customers. Bobby decides he will just look after the shareholders more than the customers — because, like he'd heard his dad say, they were clearly the most important people to the bank.

Bobby felt this could be the answer to Big Question 1: What is the *purpose* of the bank?

He decided: the bank's purpose is to make shareholders happy.

Week one, day four
Social rewards

Ms Molloy had a restless sleep last night. She knows it was only day one of the new assignment, but something about how the children were so fixated on money has left her feeling uneasy.

She can't remember children in previous years being as fixated on 'buying stuff'. Perhaps the cost of living was forcing their families into tighter financial scenarios, with no child immune to a parent's angst over money.

While discussing this with the assistant principal in the staffroom, Ms Molloy is cut short by the straight-talking Mrs Laforte.

'Your description of their banks is all about money for personal reward! And I know you better than that. I don't think this aligns with your purpose as a teacher, Bo.'

It was true. There was a danger that the students could get mixed up and think money is only for personal reward, when a truly successful capitalistic society provides social returns as well.

'How do I explain the concept of the triple bottom line to a group of eight-year-olds?' wonders Ms Molloy.

Mrs Laforte heads off to start her day. But Ms Molloy remains, her tea going cold, to redraft the paragraph about money. She needs to make sure the children understand that commercial gain is not their bank's sole prize.

When the time comes for playground duty, Ms Molloy ventures deeper into the playground and starts to think about what a bank would need to do to truly provide social returns—and what that might look like to a child.

It isn't until after the bell rings, when the kids are in their library session, that Ms Molloy can sit at her classroom desk to work out a new teaching plan to explain this lesson to the children.

Staring at a blank page, Ms Molloy imagines a world where organisations are all about purpose and going back to basics—to profit and do good. Profit for purpose, as some organisations now like to say.

But how can she impart these big business lessons around social responsibility to her young students? Drawing a big circle on the page, Ms Molloy writes a question in the centre:

'What do banks need to be if they are to be socially responsible and commercially successful?' She draws some lines coming out of the circle, topped off by three points.

1 Banks need to be *transparent*—buyers and sellers must understand the products.

2 Banks need to have a *human connection with their customers* — the relationship comes with a promise.

3 Corporations are legally protected from the type of liability that everyday people have to take on. This means they *must take great responsibility* in their decisions.

There is no doubt that her students are ready to learn the leadership lessons of transparency, honesty, courage, connectedness and responsibility. But was the link between social responsibility and commercial success going a step too far?

Getting a fresh page from her drawer and feeling more resolved, Ms Molloy draws another circle. In it she writes 'The challenges'.

Coming off from this circle, she lists a range of challenges she knows are likely to trip up her children and make them think about the link between commercial success and social responsibility.

1 How will the bankers decide who gets money, who doesn't and how much?

2 How will the bankers make sure they know their customers?

3 How much money will the bank have to lend before it is too risky?

4 Who will make sure the banks are making the right decisions and not getting out of control?

'Yep, these are good questions to ask an eight-year-old. If they get this right now, they will be set for life', thinks Ms Molloy as she puts away her sketchpad, closes the drawer and clicks off her biro tip.

If they get this right now, they will be set for life.

Back to Betsy

Ms Molloy's thoughts about the challenges banks face are interrupted by the sound of running feet. The class is back from the library and they know it is time for the assignment.

'Ms Molloy!' Betsy says, once the class has unpacked their library books and split into their groups. 'We really need your help! To find our purpose we are trying to match yesterday's "feeling" words with the New Big Words. But we have lots of leftover sad feelings that just don't fit with words like 'humanity' or 'ethical'. What do we do?'

'Okay, class', says Ms Molloy. 'Let's all stop for a moment to help Betsy's group sort through their "feeling" words as a class. We're going to look at each leftover word and Google it so we understand what it means.'

The leftover words are: frustrated, not fair, confused and stressed. Ms Molloy also writes #notnice after the naughty words. The kids are too young for Twitter but she hopes they will start to see they can use social media as a force for good when they are old enough. Baby steps.

'Okay, one word at a time. Who would like to go first?'

Nicholas's hand shoots into the air as Sally 'Swivel Neck' turns to talk to Abby. Sally is a chatty, fiercely intelligent girl who always turns in her chair to speak to her best friend, Abby, which is how she earned her nickname. Ms Molloy has lost count of the number of times Sally has spun around to explain some urgent thought she just couldn't contain.

'Okay, Sally. Which word would you like to start with?' Ms Molloy asks.

'Confused?' she says.

Sally reads the definition from Google out loud and Ms Molloy asks if anyone would want their bank to make their customers or staff feel confused. There is a big shake of the head all round, and on they go.

After they've gone through the entire list the class agrees that if they are to build a bank that goes from good to great they can't have any frustration, unfairness, confusion, stress or #notnice activities. Their purpose must actively counter this.

Betsy's group now decides they will put all the elements together— the customer's happy 'feeling' words, the New Big Words, and their concept of money—to create the answer to the first big question: What is the bank's purpose?

> The bank's purpose is to make customers happy by giving and taking money with not too much interest.

Just as the group finishes writing this statement in their exercise books, Julia points at the wall with an exasperated, louder-than-necessary sigh. 'Are we all remembering what a bank is?'

The group read the words again, silently mouthing the bigger words as they go.

Julia then asks the very pertinent question, 'Going back to the *how* here: are we saying the people who work for the bank should not have too much *interest* in *how* they do things, or are we talking about *interest*, as in money repayments to the bank?'

Everyone looks at the very proud Julia with bewilderment. But Julia is the brightest student in the class and she knows that they would not have happy customers if the people who worked for the bank didn't have much *interest* in their work.

So Julia suggests a rewrite:

> The bank's purpose is to make customers happy by giving and taking money with a little interest and to have everyone who works at the bank have lots of interest in customers.

'I think this is an excellent big-picture approach', Ms Molloy agrees, when Julia asks her to check their new purpose. She makes only a couple of changes, wishing bank's purposes could be this simple.

> The bank's purpose is to make customers happy by giving and taking money. Also to make their staff happy, as this is what will make customers happy.

She purposefully decides to leave the word *happy* in twice as she thinks there is a good lesson to be learned. And as the class starts to get restless once more, Ms Molloy claps her hands to announce her big surprise.

'Class', she announces confidently, feeling sure that her idea will help prepare her students to grapple with the intractable problems of the future. 'This afternoon, we are going to play a game I created called 'On Board' to help you learn more about organisations, the true power of money and to show you how to behave to be a great banker!'

On Board

The kids are so excited by her announcement! Usually this kind of excitement is reserved for something with a computer screen, not something handcrafted by their caring teacher. Ms Molloy is always amazed to see how much the kids love working in teams playing On Board. They strive to collect Reward cards for ethical behaviour, and unknowingly learn how all organisations (not just big business) fundamentally operate. 'Grasping the concept of ethics through play is really quite tactical', Ms Molloy thinks to herself. 'The best way for the children to apply the lessons around their bank's purpose is to live that purpose on the board', she thinks, proud of her lateral plan and the idiom which is her game's name!

Ms Molloy starts by patiently teaching her students how to play the game and explaining the role of Choice. Only one Choice card in the deck offers easy money, but lots of cards offer opportunities to do the right thing while growing your cash, and many cards teach the students that 'stuff' has to be paid for.

Next she asks them their thoughts on the object — or the purpose — of the game. Ms Molloy wants to remind the class how much purpose can influence outcomes.

Nicholas and Julia shoot their hands into the air. But Sally 'Swivel Neck' also lifts her hand, just high enough to be seen. With her neck back-to-front and centre, Sally blurts out that the object of On Board is to be the team with the most money at the end of the game.

Johnny Hehman almost punches his hand in the air to disagree. 'Uh-uh, the object is for one team to have *all* the money', he says.

'Not really', Ms Molloy replies, letting the sharp edge of frustration saturate her tone. 'Can someone who has played On Board before explain how other teams have money too?'

Julia, keenly aware of her moment to shine, puts up her hand. 'Everyone should have money in this game', she declares. 'It's just that the team with the most money *and* the most Reward cards win.'

'Thank you Julia, that is correct. How you get the money is equally important, which is why Reward cards for good ethical behaviour decide the winner', Ms Molloy says, relieved that at least her game didn't encourage Julia to be money-crazed.

Next came the part Ms Molloy was dreading: linking Big Question 1 (the *why*) with Big Question 2 (the *how*). As adults, we can see how the two combine — well, most of the time anyway — but would a class of eight-year-olds understand the link?

'Can anyone let me know how we will need to *behave* to make the game fun and also to *meet its object?*' Ms Molloy asks.

David Hehman barks out abruptly, 'That's obvious. We need to beat the other players like we do when we play ice hockey'.

Ms Molloy reminds David he must put his hand up, before asking him to describe how they behave when they play ice hockey.

'Dad says we need to do whatever it takes to win', he shrugs. 'Like, we have to play fair, follow the rules, listen to the coaches and referees, and be nice to the other team. But if we start to lose Dad tells us to *sometimes* jam the hockey stick too close to other boys' feet and to *sometimes* grab their shirts, and—'

'Thank you David, that's quite enough', interrupts Ms Molloy. 'To truly have fun and meet the object of the game, we need to behave like our New Big Words. We need to know the rules and know we can be kind to each other and still have a winning team. It's really simple and fun.'

Game time

The class returns from lunch with a bounce in their step. It is time to get on with the game.

After Bobby and Betsy agree on a banker, the two teams begin excitedly, side by side. It gets off to a good start, but it doesn't take long for the mood to shift.

'What now?' Ms Molloy wonders, only to discover that Betsy's team has lost after just five minutes! Ms Molloy lets out a sigh as she realises that the previous players hadn't shuffled the Choice cards. This meant the odds in the game had quickly become skewed; one team felt the power, but almost everyone was left paying the price!

In Bobby's team, the Hehman brothers cotton on to this too, and take advantage by misbehaving. 'Sorry, that's the hand you're dealt', they crow as they scoop up more money.

Some children now want to quit, some look like they are about to cry and others start curling their fists aggressively. It is a cocktail of bad behaviour.

As frustrating as this is for Ms Molloy, she ponders its importance. 'It's all part of Big Question 2. How do we *behave* when the game of choice affects our priorities?'

Of course, at this moment Ms Molloy, surrounded by squabbling children, has no idea that her own life will deal some unshuffled Choice cards of its own. She has no way of knowing, for example, that she will learn to live her own lesson plan and behave with grace when life takes some unexpected turns. But she *does* know it can be hard to put good intentions into action when you aren't dealt a fair hand in life, and that is the point she wants to make today.

Ms Molloy scrawls a definition on the board.

choice *(noun)*: the right, power or opportunity to choose; option

Turning around, Ms Molloy says loudly, 'Students, you have all just experienced the effect of unshuffled Choice cards. People who work in banks can sometimes experience something similar.

'Who can share with the class what we have just learned?'

'Unshuffled Choice cards let us win without getting in trouble because shuffling is not written in the rules', David Hehman barks.

'I'm sure many adults would agree with you there', Ms Molloy thinks, remembering the heated phone call she'd made last week on behalf of her elderly neighbour, Jeff, who had been fined for not answering the door to an electrician. Despite Ms Molloy's phone calls, the company kept citing their policy without compassion.

'Thank you, David', she says, vowing to visit her neighbour again tonight to 'shuffle those cards'.

Ms Molloy continues: 'The thing about rules is that sometimes they cannot explain all the smaller details in life—or worse still, they are understood but not followed or shared. When dealt a wild card or a hand that is just not fair, we have to choose what the right thing to do is.'

'Right', Ms Molloy says, switching tack while she has their attention. 'Let's have all eyes to the front of the room to read about our New Big Word "ethical" again.'

ethical *(adjective)*: relating to right and wrong behaviour

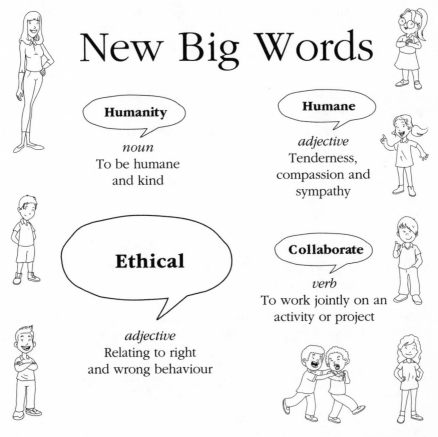

New Big Words

Humanity

noun
To be humane
and kind

Humane

adjective
Tenderness,
compassion and
sympathy

Ethical

adjective
Relating to right
and wrong behaviour

Collaborate

verb
To work jointly on an
activity or project

'Being ethical means that we have to decide between right and wrong. We know in our hearts that the Choice cards should always be shuffled, even if the rules don't say that. That way, everyone gets a fair chance.

'So to be ethical we need to choose right over wrong even if the rules don't agree or don't tell us to. Choosing makes you the leader of your life!'

'Does anyone else have any ideas about how we need to behave in our bank?' she asks, pointing at Big Question 2 as a reminder.

For the first time in a while, Betsy chirps up. 'We need to remember all those "feeling" words that people mentioned when describing the bank. We should behave in a way that makes people feel good and happy, even when difficult choices come our way', she says, starting strong but growing a little less confident as she continues.

Ms Molloy is thrilled. 'Great work, Betsy! And remember, choice gives us the opportunity to be ethical and make the right decisions. Hard sometimes, but it will lead you to win even if it doesn't feel that way at the time.'

Betsy beams with joy as the class falls quiet. Ms Molloy allows the kids to absorb the double-dealing concept of choice while she quickly shuffles the cards.

She decides to supervise the team and the banker so they can all get out of this game intact. She giggles to herself, 'If only I was supervising during the GFC'.

Whenever Ms Molloy is halfway through an exercise, she likes to do a floor walk to see how everyone is doing and make sure they are working to the purpose of the exercise.

'After all, you've got to inspect what you expect!'

As she walks around to make sure the children are working to the purpose of the exercise, Ms Molloy hears disgruntled tones over at Bobby's team and she strides over to investigate.

Bobby divulges a detailed account under the pressure of Ms Molloy's authoritative presence. 'Um, well, the Hehman brothers remembered the Whistleblower rule and instead of using the Disclosure cards to share their organisation's information formally or with a blog, they only told us boys.'

Looking steadily at Bobby's pink cheeks, Ms Molloy decides to give Bobby's team some feedback. 'Team, it is important that we all play fairly. Why have the girls in your team not received the information and the boys have? It's not fair for the girls to have to lean in to be informed. And if I see on your Disclosure card correctly, I believe both teams should have been told?'

The students stare at the table and avoid eye contact. 'And why did you think the Whistleblower rule means not to share information?' Ms Molloy created this extra rule just for this lesson of knowing the importance of when and what to disclose.

'But Ms Molloy', David Hehman whines. 'I'm just trying to win. I want as much cash as possible ...' Ms Molloy jumps in: 'Remember On Board is played in teams. The team wins or nobody wins.' Ms Molloy quietly points to the New Big Word, Collaboration.

Ms Molloy, a woman of height and stature, gives David one of her 'looks', takes a deep breath and remembers her conversation with Mrs Laforte: *A successful capitalist society provides social returns as well.*

It was a good reminder. What better social returns could there be than to help children learn important leadership lessons?

Determined to teach the concept of transparency before the day is out, she walks to the front of the class, claps everyone to attention and gives them the five-minute warning.

'Class, I think we all learned lessons about how we need to *be* to play the game fairly', she says calmly, once the children have packed up On Board and settled back in their seats. 'If you imagine your bank is like the game we just played, what would you have learned?'

At that, Julia leaps up in her seat and strains her arm in the air: a relieved Ms Molloy gives Julia a warm smile for her effort. 'Yes, Julia?'

'If our bank was like how we played our game, you would make sure we knew the object of the game, knew the rules and played by the rules. You also would remember how to behave if you were ever faced with an important choice along the way.'

'Excellent, Julia! We also learned a great deal by looking at Bobby's team', Ms Molloy adds. 'Sometimes when we want to win too badly, it is tempting to not play by the rules—probably because we are scared of losing. It's easy to forget to be ethical.

'But if some people play by different rules it makes the game very complicated and some teams don't understand why they are losing', she continues. 'Those who knew the extra rules used this hidden knowledge to help them win more, even if it wasn't transparent—even in their own team.

'But when we all take responsibility and accountability for what we are doing, everyone can see we are all playing by the same rules. It helps the people who run the game to be more trusted and have more people want to play with them. This way, we always get a better, fairer outcome.

'I'm wondering, class', continues Ms Molloy. 'If you were going to create On Board from scratch and write the object and purpose, would you keep it as it is?'

Nicholas's hand hovers gingerly in the air. 'Ms Molloy I think the Whistleblower rule should be part of the game for everyone, and is a bit … confusing.'

'Can you explain why it is confusing, Nicholas?' Ms Molloy asks with heartfelt sincerity. 'Here is a boy who is really connected with his heart', she thinks, approvingly. 'What would you change in the Whistleblower rule?'

Glancing at the New Big Words that Ms Molloy had stuck on the wall, Nicholas says, 'What about: the Whistleblower rule is to use Disclosure cards to share information that you think people should know about so we are collaborating and being ethical?'

'Unbelievable', thinks Ms Molloy. 'I love that kid.'

With the sound of the recess bell going, Ms Molloy quickly adds, 'Nicholas what a great idea for everyone to consider! And last but not least, I loved that both teams trusted your banker and that your banker could be trusted! Now let's pack up and go off to recess.'

Ms Molloy feels good but tired after her morning; it is time to have an easy afternoon. She asks everyone to take turns reading their chapter books before the final bell rings and class is dismissed.

Week one, day five
Bank names

While walking to school this morning, Ms Molloy decides she will let the class name their banks. She wants to do this early on, because she remembers from previous years that the naming session can end in tears when the children are tired.

'I swear if a cartoon character features one more time I will have to walk out of the room', she thinks to herself as she walks past the oak tree and through the school gate. 'Or those blasted video games. They always have names that promote violence.'

It is the last day of their first week and the children now know where to put their bags and homework. Very shortly they are sitting on the mat waiting for Ms Molloy to start the class.

'Good morning class.' Ms Molloy smiles at the little people who are wiping sleep out of their eyes.

'One of your tasks today is to name your bank, and it needs to be a group decision. I want you to think of a creative name that reflects your bank's purpose. Do not bring me a name from a movie, video game or TV show', she says, in a voice more stern than intended. 'Remember everyone has an equal part in naming your bank, and there is to be no calling out.

'If your idea is not selected, please continue to participate—no moping about.

'Yes, I am looking at you two', Ms Molloy says, facing the Hehman brothers. 'You really did not collaborate when we named our tables on Monday, so no nonsense from you please.'

Just as Ms Molloy finishes, David blows a big bubble with banned bubblegum. 'Spit that out now David!' she says, suddenly wishing she could step back in time to last year's holiday in Barbados.

'And please, make sure it makes sense for a bank', Ms Molloy continues, holding a tissue out for David to spit his gum into, her mood descending just a touch as she puts it in the trash.

'We need a bloody name', she thinks to herself. 'But the idea of choosing just one name can really show the horrible side of humanity.' She remembers the many snotty tears that fell last year when groups could not agree.

'Okay, split up into your groups please and remember to take turns listening to each other', Ms Molloy says, sitting down at her desk.

At this, Betsy approaches her desk. 'Ms Molloy, does it matter if we all don't agree?'

'Try to get some agreement', says Ms Molloy impatiently.

Ms Molloy doesn't even realise she is the one getting the most flustered, letting patterns from previous years dictate how she behaves today. Sometimes even teachers need to go back to school for a day.

Eventually the children settle into a rhythm and seem to be working well together. Shortlists are being made and much enthusiastic nodding is going on.

Ms Molloy gives the five-minute warning. 'Betsy and Bobby, please write the name of your bank on your paper, get everyone to sign the back and then come to the front to present it.'

Bobby rushes to the front and begins before Ms Molloy can say anything. He holds it up to her proudly:

The Big Bubblegum Bank

Bobby is beaming. A defeated sigh escapes Ms Molloy as she chews the name over in her mind, 'It's the end of day and I'm going to let this one slide', she thinks.

'And please do tell us how you came up with that name', she says.

'We want our bank to be so big that if it makes any mistakes everything will be okay', he says.

'Do you mean *too big to fail*, Bobby?'

'Yes!' he shouts, and goes to high-five his classmates, who mostly miss and hit each other's earlobes.

'And the rest, Bobby? Why Bubblegum?' asks Ms Molloy.

'Well the Hehmans like bubblegum, and their dad talked about bubbles bursting when they had to sell their house, so we thought this meant bubblegum can be an adult thing too.

'So we are the Big Bubblegum Bank!'

'Okay. Well, that is a lot to say in one go, so I will refer to it as BBG, if that's okay?'

'Okay!' Bobby says, really excited that Ms Molloy let them keep the name even though you are not supposed to have gum in class. It is so scandalous!

'Okay, Betsy. Now hop to the front quickly before the bell rings.'

Betsy walks with grace to the front of the room; she feels her group's name is so perfect and she wants to enjoy this moment. She holds up the name:

The Bank of Humanity

Ms Molloy is happier than a branding agency at the start of a new big contract. 'What a perfect name', she thinks to herself.

'Wonderful, Betsy. Thank you for including one of our New Big Words. I will refer to your bank as BoH.

'Now, leaders please have someone in your group create a picture with your bank's name on it. Be as creative as you like; we will work on these during art and computer time.'

And so comes the sweet sound of the bell to mark the start of recess and signal the start of other work for the day. Ms Molloy is already looking forward to next week, though the thought of a lazy weekend ahead is more than welcome, too.

Week two, day one

Candy jar

Ms Molloy wakes up in her simple but well-kept town house, excited that the heat has started to ease off and the autumn weather is settling in. She loves the changing colour of the leaves, the cosy sweaters and scarves, and drinking her favourite pumpkin-flavoured coffee from her thermos.

As the bell rings for the start of another day, the children take some time to settle down. They always get excited around this time of year, with Halloween and Thanksgiving just around the corner and

Santa swiftly following. Many teachers bemoan this busy time of year, but Ms Molloy has always loved its spirit of festivity.

Keen for things to begin, she starts clapping to quiet the class. Sure enough, the children start clapping back to the same beat until not a single mouth is uttering a word.

'Good morning class!' Ms Molloy says in the bright, ringing voice that she adopts when she wants to really motivate the students. It doesn't come naturally to her, but once she copied the tone from a friend she understood how much power it could hold. 'Today we are going to look at the next element of our assignment, and it has something to do with … candy!'

The class gasps, like these are the best words they have ever heard on a Monday morning. And maybe they are. But Ms Molloy knows there is more to this treat than meets the eye. She got the idea from her mother, Peggy Molloy, and has experienced its important lessons firsthand.

Peggy grew up tumbling around the wet green hills of Ireland, and believes children should be brought up with openness, responsibility and boundaries between right and wrong. So when Peggy moved her family to America, she packed the Irish Lolly Jar, along with its important lessons. Its name changed when they settled in America, but its purpose remained the same.

The idea was simple. The big glass jar would sit in the middle of the table, and wait there in all its glory. Everyone could see the bright pops of colour nestled inside, and everyone could see if someone had taken a greedy handful. Sneaky dips into the jar were always noticed; things were transparent and tracked.

Importantly, everyone knew the treats inside the jar were only for exceptional behaviour. You were only rewarded when you did something deserving.

With childhood candy jar life-lessons filling her mind, Ms Molloy had eagerly rapped on the office door of her opinionated principal, Mrs Doogan, the week before. Together they had sat in the small and exceptionally organised office as she explained her idea.

The stubborn principal had stared at Ms Molloy for a while, before agreeing to allow the candy jar. Ms Molloy was stunned! Of course, the risk assessment paperwork was endless. There were choking risks, allergy awareness sheets and the sugar content to consider—not to mention the note that she would have to write and send home to the parents. Wow.

Mrs Doogan had just one proviso: she insisted on being in the classroom when the candy jar was presented to the class. She wanted to ensure that everyone, including Ms Molloy, understood how special it is to receive a candy jar as part of class. Normally she would have said no, but Mrs Doogan had experienced the effect of greed firsthand when she was a child, and wanted to stamp it out of children wherever she could. She loved the metaphor of the transparent candy jar as the banker's bonus... but she was careful to keep her delight to herself. She didn't want Ms Molloy getting too carried away with her continual extra-curricular requests.

Today, when Mrs Doogan swings open the classroom door to honour the class with her presence, the children quickly fall silent and sit extra straight. Ms Molloy can't help but be frustrated that life still runs off hierarchy, and tensely announces that Mrs Doogan is here to share something special with the class.

Gleefully, Mrs Doogan shares the privilege. 'Class, it is my pleasure to let you know that Ms Molloy has organised for you to have a candy jar as part of your assignment', she says. Immediately there are more gasps, and bodies start to shuffle in chairs.

Mrs Doogan puts a stern hand in the air to call for silence before anyone has even uttered word. 'I have agreed to this for one reason: this candy jar is no ordinary candy jar. It is here to represent something called a 'bonus'. This is your reward when you as bankers do extra work to create a great bank.

'It's important that you don't just think about the candy jar the whole time', she says. 'You must focus on the purpose of your assignment.'

'Can anyone think of a way we can all get back to the task at hand so the candy bonus isn't the only thing motivating us here?', Ms Molloy asks, keen to show her class's understanding in action.

Betsy's hand flies in the air and Mrs Doogan picks her to speak.

'I think we need to put it away so we can't see it, otherwise we will always be doing things just to get the candy and impress the owner of the jar, instead of answering the four very important Big Questions and getting on with our jobs', says Betsy with great confidence.

She is sure people try to impress the bonus owners, because she often hides behind the study door at home to listen to her mother's conference calls.

Her mum, Vikki, is a single mother who works very hard. She always says things like 'they are just doing that to get their bonuses', 'they don't care about customers, only their bonuses' and 'they're too busy looking after their bonuses to look after their staff'.

'Excellent, Betsy!' says the wiry-haired principal. She plonks the large glass container in the centre of Ms Molloy's wooden desk. Excitable disbelief charges through the class and, with that, Mrs Doogan sweeps out the room.

'So, class, here is the story behind the candy jar. When I was growing up, my mother would give us treats from our candy jar whenever we did extra special things. They had to be things that made everyone in our house happy — not just ourselves', Ms Molloy explains carefully.

The lesson she wants to share is that greed is *not* good, and neither is popping your hand into the candy jar when no-one is looking or trying to impress the owner of the candy jar just so you get a piece!

'Betsy and Bobby, as the leaders, you are going to have to decide who gets candy, when they get candy and how much they get, to be approved by me upon collection', says Ms Molloy, charging on with the task at hand.

'It will be just like running a company. Did you know that many companies give the people who work with them a bonus — just like our candy? It's something extra on top of their salary, and it's there to say thank-you when people do things that help make their companies great.

'Not everyone gets one, and it seems there is never enough to go around, but that's another story', she says, thinking there are only so many adult lessons you can teach a class of eight-year-olds.

Ms Molloy looks around the class and is happy to see they are all paying attention, with eyes stuck to her as she waves a fistful of paper in the air. 'I want everyone to take one of these permission slips home so your parents know about the candy jar', she says, handing them out one by one. 'Your homework is to discuss with your parents what kinds of things they would like you, their bankers, to do to make a great bank, and therefore get a bonus — like candy.'

Ms Molloy makes a mental note not to expect the parents to become too involved, as that would conflict with her purpose by disadvantaging children whose parents aren't very hands-on.

'But I still don't understand how we'll know who gets the candy', Sally says, interrupting Ms Molloy's thoughts.

'You can make lists of all the things you are doing in your bank that make it great', Ms Molloy continues calmly. 'Then if you get lots of them done you will get a candy bonus.

'Most importantly, all the things you do should reflect your purpose — including *how* you do them.'

Bobby knows straightaway what this means and says, 'I think *everyone* in the team should get a treat now. That's the fairest thing'.

'But then you may be too busy enjoying your treats to do your important work!' Ms Molloy says, closing the idea down before continuing with the lesson.

'Class, can someone explain how the candy fits in with our Big Questions?' She looks around expectantly, and empty faces stare back at her.

'Here they are again', Ms Molloy says, switching on the Smartboard.

1 What is the *purpose* of the bank?

2 How will people at the bank need to *behave*?

3 What will the people at the bank need to *do*?

4 What will you need to do to make the bank *work*?

Silence. Just when Ms Molloy thinks this is too complicated for children, Julia pops up her hand.

'Ms Molloy', she says, eyes wide and unblinking. 'Our group now has a purpose for our bank. And then we learned from playing On Board how we have to *behave*... sooo, if we remember these two things when we work out the answers to Big Questions 3 and 4... will we get candy? Err, I mean a bonus?'

Impressed, Ms Molloy says, 'That was an outstanding summary Julia! When working on all the Big Questions, ask yourself: what would make your bank go from good to great so that you get a nice treat for your hard work?

'It's like when you get treats at home. Can anyone share what you need to do to make this happen?'

At this, Johnny Hehman pops up out of his seat. 'Our dad gives me an extra hour on the X-Box if I put my shoes and school bag on the shelf near the front door to make him less stressed in the morning!'

'Really?' asks Nicholas, incredulously. 'My parents say that's just the way we are supposed to behave. They only give me treats when I do something *extra* special.'

Now David chimes in and says to his brother, 'But Johnny, Dad always gives us treats as long as we help him do the things *he* is supposed to do'.

'Okay class', Ms Molloy interrupts. 'Remember to speak with your parents about rewards, and the candy jar, and please give them the note.' Time for recess — and for other more conventional curriculum to take over for the rest of the day.

Week two, day two
Parental participation
'Good morning everyone!' Ms Molloy says in a bright voice that sounds like birds and bells.

'I am excited to get back to our assignment and find out how everyone is going', she announces. 'But remember, purpose comes first!

'So, Betsy and Bobby, can you please both come to the front of the class and remind everybody what the purpose of your bank is?'

Betsy leaps up to the front of the class while Bobby follows at a much slower pace. In turn, they read their purposes from the whiteboard: Betsy confident and sprightly, Bobby quiet and sullen.

'Bobby, your presentation makes it sound like you're not very happy about your purpose', says Ms Molloy. 'Why is that?'

Bobby looks at her and hesitates. 'I think I need to speak with my dad again about why we need the shareholders to be happy', he replies quietly.

'Why is that, Bobby?' asks Ms Molloy, pleased that he is starting to question his purpose. Bobby starts to stammer, so Ms Molloy checks herself and gives him the slow-down sign.

'I think I like Betsy's group's purpose better...' he says in a barely audible voice.

With a mental high-five, Ms Molloy thinks this is a great time to introduce the next phase of her plan—getting the parents more involved in the class assignment. Ms Molloy sneakily gets the parents to guide and coach rather than do the work. So funny how she is coaching the parents to understand the importance of helping rather than doing *and* teaching the class about the role of regulators in banking!

'Well, Bobby, why don't you talk to your dad about your group's purpose? Then you can share your answers tomorrow in show-and-tell.

'You could invite your dad to come visit our class too, if you would like', Ms Molloy says, voicing a thought she'd had the night before. 'He could really help everyone learn more about banks.'

Bobby springs to life and grins a toothy grin. 'That's a great idea', he yells. 'I'll ask him tonight!'

Ms Molloy raises her voice to finish her sentence before his excitement takes hold. 'Tell your dad I will give him a call if he decides he can do this so we can talk through the assignment.' She had sat through a lot of 'off-message' parent presentations in her career; the last thing she needed now was someone who would confuse the class.

'Now, let's talk about why it is important to have rules and regulations. When I wanted to include a candy jar in our assignment I knew that I had to follow the school rules, which say that I have to ask permission. That's why I asked our Mrs Doogan. Mrs Doogan is responsible for making sure that we are following the rules, and to make sure the rules make sense and are achieving their purpose. Does everyone understand?'

The class agrees. 'So why do we have rules about the candy jar bonus, for example?' asks Ms Molloy.

The silence pushes her onward. 'Well, there are a few reasons. Take allergies, for example. One of our rules helps make sure that all the candy at the school is free from nuts. And by obeying this rule we are keeping everyone safe and happy.'

'That doesn't make sense', David shouts out. 'People aren't allergic to money, Ms Molloy!'

'Put up your hand David', she says, before continuing with her lesson. 'Not many people are allergic to money, no. But similar to our school, banks need other people to check their work — because many people rely on banks to take care of their money.' She sighs.

'Can someone think of an example of the kind of help a bank would need?' Ms Molloy presses on, choosing Sally to share the answer and stop her mid-swivel en route to her best friend Abby.

Sally is startled but prepared. 'I think someone needs to check that the money is in the bank, like the bank says it is.'

'Excellent point, Sally. There are a few people who check on banks — the accountants, the government and the regulators. They all check in a slightly different way but they all play a role in making sure the bank is working the way it should be.'

Betsy pops her hand up. 'I get it, Ms Molloy! The regulator for banks is like when my mother has to get her car checked to make sure it is okay to drive.

'I love when we do that because she lets me turn on the lights!' she says, feeling very responsible and trusted indeed.

'Exactly, Betsy. Great example', Ms Molloy agrees. 'If only it were that simple', she thinks.

'So now that we understand who "checks" our bank, I thought it would be fun to ask your parents to help out with this', Ms Molloy tells her class, knowing full well that some of them will be 'helping' already. 'We will work through our Big Questions 3 and 4 and then we will get your parents to check up on what your bank is doing!'

The bell rings for recess and a hungry stampede exits the room, breaking all rules and regulations about walking slowly indoors. 'Baby steps', Ms Molloy thinks to herself as she heads to the staffroom.

Back to the *how*

Ms Molloy spent most of recess photocopying a note for the children to hand to their parents. Now back in the classroom, holding the warm papers fresh from the photocopier, Ms Molloy starts handing out the notes as she speaks.

'When you get home today, give your parents this note. Ask them to help you highlight any items on your list that they think someone would need to check', she says.

'We want our banks to inspect the things we expect, which is why we want your parents to be the regulators. They help make sure your banks are being ethical.'

'Now, Betsy and Bobby, I would like you to get your groups together and share ideas on Question 3 — the things you think people in a bank would need to do, *how* to make your purpose happen.'

At the sound of the lunch bell, Ms Molloy dashes again to the staffroom. She knows Mr Aitkens will be in there on a Tuesday because that is when the teachers bring cakes in to school and it spices up his week. She plans on talking to Mr Aitkens about whether he would like to join classes next term for a few sessions, in the hope she can freshen up his style without offending him.

Despite her good intentions, she ends up sitting at the big staffroom table after the cakes have been devoured, once again engrossed writing in her sketchpad.

Ms Molloy wants to turn the four Big Questions into a visual learning guide for the class. 'I need diagrams. Maybe even an acronym', she thinks, as she starts doodling words on the page. No sooner has she decided to do this than the bell rings and it's time to get stuck back into the cut and thrust of the day ahead.

Week two, day three

No time

Today is brisk, so after breakfast Ms Molloy pops on her favourite new circle scarf, the one that keeps the chill from her neck but never gets in her way when she leans over desks. Perfect.

She looks forward to hearing from a (hopefully) more confident Bobby in show-and-tell.

Bobby is indeed first into class as the bell rings. 'Very unusual', thinks Ms Molloy.

'Ms Molloy?' he stands at the door uncertainly. 'My dad is so busy that he can't speak to me until Thursday night about coming into class but he did talk to me about purpose. Is it okay if I ask him about coming into class later on?' Bobby asks, disappointment tugging at the corners of his mouth.

'Of course you can', Ms Molloy replies and smiles warmly.

'I wonder if parents realise the impact of time in a fleeting childhood', she thinks to herself as Bobby smiles back and unpacks his bag. 'If only we decided how much time we want in life, how much it would cost to have that time and then worked to that plan!' Ms Molloy wonders if she is being fair. She hasn't really given him much notice. 'Sometimes we—I—judge too quickly', she thinks.

The rest of the class trickles in, with excitement of the end of the week nearing in the air. The class bubbles with chatter as they wait to hear from Bobby, who is holding a box of chocolates and sitting patiently on the mat.

'Right then', Ms Molloy starts. 'Up you come, Bobby. We are all keen to hear from you!'

Always one to set her students up to succeed, she reminds Bobby of the topic before he begins. 'So you are going to share your chat with your dad about when bankers should get a candy bonus? And to check your group's purpose makes sense, is that right Bobby?'

'That's right, Ms Molloy', Bobby says, coughing nervously as he approaches the front of the class, clutching the box of chocolates in his sweaty hand.

'Good morning class', says Bobby.

'Good—morning—Bobby', replies the class.

'For show-and-tell today I want to talk about why people should get a bonus, or in our case a piece of candy.

'My dad said if our candy is the bonus for our bankers at the Big Bubblegum Bank then it should only be given to the people who do what they said they are going to do—and who behave like they say they are going to. The better you are, the more candy you get.'

'Interesting', thinks Ms Molloy, who always had an inkling that Bob had had a good head on his shoulders many years ago, before financial pressure and time constraints changed him.

'He also said that some companies make the candy bonus available only if you go through what he called a 'gate opener'. This is like the gate to the playground, he said. It's there to keep the bank safe, just like the gate at the playground.

'Dad also said that at some companies making a lot of money can be the gate opener.' Bobby pauses, confused, and looks at Ms Molloy, who nods encouragingly.

'Next I gave my dad the four Big Questions. He liked them a lot. He said the people who can remember to link purpose, behaviour, what and how they do things will get the candy. And the better they do them, the more candy they get.

'My dad also said bonuses are like a box of chocolates — you never know what you might get. He laughed at that bit a lot so I think that's quite important, though he said it in a funny accent, said something about the forest and some gump, but I didn't get the joke.'

Ms Molloy sighs on the inside and smiles sweetly on the outside. Does everyone think in movie references these days? Mind you, she often thought in book titles, so she shouldn't really judge.

'Then he got serious again and said there are only so many chocolates in the box — meaning that some people don't ever get bonuses. He said they get a donut.'

'A donut?' Ms Molloy asks, her eyebrows shooting up.

'Not a real donut, Dad said. They don't get any candy. I didn't understand that bit either to be honest.'

'Hmm', Ms Molloy accidentally says out loud, knowing precisely that what Bob meant is a big fat zero!

'That was great, Bobby! Now does anyone have any questions for Bobby about why, who, when and how much candy gets given out as a bonus?'

'Because that's where bonus allocations get sticky', she thinks to herself, reflecting on the horror stories of her friends in corporate roles. 'Almost as sticky as those sugar-coated donuts', she chuckles inwardly.

The class mostly agrees that the bonuses are to be handed out fair and square (apart from the usual naysayers at the back) and so they go back to Bobby's show-and-tell.

'Okay Bobby. So how did you go with your dad on your group's purpose?' Ms Molloy asks.

'Well, my dad started pointing to all the papers from his bank again, so I showed him our purpose. He said it had only been a couple of weeks since we created the Big Bubblegum Bank's purpose and that he didn't say anything at the time, but that he thinks the days of thinking only of shareholders are over.

'My dad went to his bookshelf and picked out lots of books.' Here Bobby checks himself and turns to pick up all the books he had placed at the front of the class earlier on in a clumsy fashion. He shows them to the class before putting them on Ms Molloy's desk and picking up a piece of paper to read from.

'Dad handed these books to me and said, "The days of hardball are over. It's time to start fixing the game, and get back to basics, just as Peter Drucker says in his books".

'Then he said that our bank needs to have more in its purpose than just the shareholders.'

Bobby now grabs his palm cards out of his pocket and asks Ms Molloy for permission to read from them so he doesn't miss anything. Ms Molloy agrees, as she is excited by where this is going—even though she prefers show-and-tell to be memorised.

'You do not have a business without a customer', he reads. 'The customer matters. It is the customer's willingness to buy what you have that keeps your organisation going. So we must have the customer at the centre of our purpose.'

'Wow, thank you Bobby!' says Ms Molloy. 'It sounds like you and your dad had some quality time together last night, and you certainly answered both questions, thank you. Class, let's give Bobby a hand', she says, and they do, obligingly.

'So Bobby', Ms Molloy continues. 'You and your group need to meet in our next session to decide what your new purpose will be, based on this information.

'Betsy, you can review your original purpose and then start working on what your bank needs to *do*, Big Question 3, to make sure it supports this purpose.'

As the recess bell goes, Ms Molloy feels her shoulders lighten a little. The rest of the week is the light material, she vows to herself as the weekend draws close.

Week two, weekend

PLOT

Ms Molloy always leaves her Sunday nights free to prepare for the school week ahead. Often snuggled up with a cup of tea or glass of red, she enjoys the calm that quiet preparation brings. She is a far more committed teacher than you might expect; a vivacious woman with her friends, she always connects her head and heart through her work. It's a commitment drenched in social returns, because she knows the value of the children, her customers, goes beyond a pay slip.

Ms Molloy picks up her notepad and looks at the mind map she doodled the other day.

She starts to make out a four-leaf clover from the mess of marks she had made. She smiles. Her mother Peggy loves shamrocks and the notion of Irish luck, and Ms Molloy herself has had hours of teacher training with many a clover-filled diagram.

Imagining the clover, Ms Molloy breaks down the concept of actualising purpose into the first, most obvious, leaf: know your purpose. She draws a big P in the top left leaf and scribbles the first Big Question next to it, while considering the New Big Words' impact on the outcome.

'I wonder how anyone can connect with a company's purpose if they are not clear on their own personal purpose', she thinks. But she quickly disregards that thought to focus on creating this graphic for her young class. 'Let's keep things simple', she tells herself.

'Just assume the organisation's purpose connects with people's personal purpose.'

In her own life, Ms Molloy already knows her behaviour as a teacher has to reflect her personal purpose. In this sense, she matches Big Question 1 with Big Question 2 every single day to make sure her values at home and work align. She knows she will be the one to suffer eventually if they don't.

As part of this ongoing process, Ms Molloy strives to create awareness in the children that she teaches. She wants to help them understand who they are, so they can begin to express themselves authentically and more powerfully, instead of mirroring the behaviour of friends or, worse, those twerking idols on TV.

Ms Molloy doesn't always see what a big impact this has on the students lucky enough to pass through her classroom each year, but she continues all the same, largely unaware of the enormous influence she has on the lives she is shaping for the long term.

'Why can't everyone see themselves as leaders?' she wonders as she focuses on the clover once more. Leaders come from anywhere; you certainly don't have to have followers to be a leader.

To *be* is the most important concept of Big Question 2, she knows. But to be what?

'To be a leader', Ms Molloy thinks. 'To be a leader is simply how we behave. L for leader. And a purpose-led leader at that. Because when you link it to the Big Words, the children can see what those behaviours should be — humane and ethical.'

She draws an L for leadership next to the P, and scribbles Big Question 2 next to it, before moving on to Big Question 3 — the things the bank would need to *do*.

For this, she writes a list of tasks that any bank would need to do to deliver its products and services. And, as the list grows longer, she searches her mind for a word that will tie them all together, all of these details and actions and activities. Popping online, Ms Molloy stumbles on a definition she likes.

operation *(noun)*: the power to act; efficacy, influence, or force

'Perfect', she thinks. 'It shows us achieving purpose requires action, it highlights the need for leadership through influence, and it covers the need for command and control from time to time. That's what every teacher learns about very early on as well!'

Writing an O in the lower left leaf and scribbling Big Question 3 beside it, she moves on to the final leaf in the clover.

Big Question 4 looms large: what does everyone need?

But just then Ms Molloy is interrupted by her mum texting to ask if she would like to FaceTime chat. She chuckles: 'Daft woman still doesn't understand that she can just FaceTime me like she would call me!' Grabbing her phone, Ms Molloy stares at its grubby screen. 'Surely technology is the backbone of every bank', she thinks as she unlocks it. 'It connects our world, it transforms and disrupts markets!'

A huge grin spreads across the often-serious face of Ms Molloy.

Purpose. **L**eadership. **O**perations. **T**echnology.

'PLOT!' she thinks. 'Bingo!' as she writes the T down in the final leaf of the clover and scribbles Big Question 4 beside it. Her mum would have to wait a moment.

Ms Molloy knows the children will never forget those bloody Big Questions again. The concept of plot is already so infused in their lives, which are full of TV shows, movies and books! It is music to Ms Molloy's ears.

Bobby's house

Every Sunday night at Bobby's house the family has dinner together, after which Bob retreats to his home office to prepare for his week, just like Ms Molloy. Before he leaves, they have a Sunday night ritual of sharing their week's highs and lows.

Bobby cannot contain himself and begs to go first. 'My high was on Wednesday night with Dad in his study. He taught me so many things about how to share money, how banks need to look after customers and he helped me choose my things for show-and-tell which went so well!' he says through mouthfuls of mashed potato.

'Then my next high was Thursday at school. My show-and-tell was one of the best ever, Ms Molloy said. I knew it was good because all the kids were quiet and Sally didn't even swivel once!'

'That's great, Bobby!' his dad says. 'Any lows?'

Out pops a loud and happy 'no' from Bobby. Bob is surprised and even a little moved. He knows Bobby can be naturally pessimistic at times and it is beautiful to see his eyes sparkle.

After dinner, Bob excuses himself to prepare for his early morning trip to Chicago, where important industry analysts are waiting to bend his ear. He closes his door, slumps into his leather chair and swings back and forth—straight back into work mode.

'I am the man in the middle', he thinks. 'I am the guy sitting between capital markets and product markets.'

'That is it.' He sits up. 'It's time to focus on our customers more.'

Bob always vowed to work hard so he could provide for his family. But being the hero achiever in a large family is not always easy. He has known that for a long time. He was raised by his mother on a secretary's salary while his father laboured hard as an ironworker—and then tipped his earnings down his neck after work. It was all before he was old enough to understand the different forms of domestic violence, but even then he knew it was not exactly meaningful fathering.

He decided hard work was his ticket out, so he worked until the sun went down and the pens dried out at university. His studious life in Connecticut had been a turning point—until he was forced to return home due to his terrible financial situation, which was now also burdened with student loans. So he took the first job he could and started in the local branch office. He has worked his way through the ranks, and he has made it. He is now on Wall Street and is apparently living the dream he has always had.

'Or have I made it? I never have much time for family or fun, and I'm pretty sure I'm becoming more bitter as the days go on', he thinks, his thumbs now kneading his chin absent-mindedly.

When Bob needs time out to think, he likes to visit their white, stilted beach house on Long Beach Island (reverently known as LBI to those in the know), with its minty-green trim that has been honoured in upkeep by generations.

His picture-perfect beach house on LBI, New Jersey, is where Bob goes to sort out his corporate troubles, and the irony is not lost on him. Knowing he needs to finish closing up the house for winter, he decides he will spend the upcoming weekend alone in the township of Loveladies, LBI, after his trip to Chicago.

We leave Ms Molloy packing away her sketchpad, and we leave Bobby and his mum packing the dishwasher to travel forward in time with Bob to the weekend ahead.

Week three, weekend

Long Beach Island

Bob spends Saturday at the beach house immersed in the ritual of packing, sweeping, wiping and cleaning, and enjoys seeing order take shape before him. Then, keen to stretch out his aching muscles, he decides to take a run to Barnegat Lighthouse.

Barnegat Lighthouse is the second tallest lighthouse in the whole of the United States and, more importantly, it's Bob's favourite lighthouse in the entire world. He has a penchant for the solid, old-fashioned structures—the history, the engineering, and the architecture that stoically remains, no matter how many waves crash against its foundations. The lighthouse remains the same as it was when he was a boy, and Bob takes a deep comfort in that unchanging world.

Last year he used his bonus to pay for a family trip-of-a-lifetime, as he called it, from London to Singapore to Australia. It was unheard-of to take a four-week holiday in July and so Bob worked with his old high school buddy Peter to make sure the trip was planned just right.

Peter is a travel agent whose business thrives, in spite of online travel alternatives, because he focuses on his customers. It's a personal skill Bob is sure comes naturally, but Peter tells Bob he has to consciously make sure he is not in 'task mode' with his customers.

As a regular yoga student (unusual for the blue-collar neighbourhood in which he lives), Peter also meditates daily, and says the practice helps him set his intention each day. He wants to be with his customers and *know* the person. All any customer really wants is to feel understood, and so Peter sets up systems and time to make this his job every day.

It's all a bit quirky for Bob, to be frank, but he looks past the process because he loves the outcome. Take Bob's love of lighthouses, for example. Peter knew, Peter remembered, and Peter effortlessly infused those beautifully solid structures into the trip schedule! Who would have thought they would get to compare British, Asian, and Australian lighthouses! In Australia they travelled from the lighthouse in Norah Head, with its Latin motto meaning 'once perilous, now safe', to end up at the iconic Byron Bay lighthouse.

Today he arrives at Barnegat Lighthouse (or Old Barney, as the locals call it), feeling glad for the run but tired.

Stopping at the base, he looks up at the 165-foot (50-metre) tower and feels a wonderful peace settle around him. It feels good because he hasn't been able to shake the feeling of emptiness all week — the feeling of something missing, something not quite right. But here, it seems to quieten down in the presence of something much more grounded and timeless.

He knows he is a good family man — based on his recent leadership training — he knows his values. They are: financial security, professional growth, control, reward and, of course, family.

'But what is it all for?' Bob asks himself. 'Is helping my family really doing enough?' The weight of his determination to be a better man than his father continues to press on his shoulders.

'And even if that is my purpose, am I doing it enough? I have the family budget nailed, but do I ever budget the *time*? Or is it all about my money and what we have?'

His emotions threaten to spill over. Bob sucks in some salty ocean air and looks up. 'Remember the lighthouse', he tells himself. 'We all need direction and we all need to be safe. I have focused a lot on safety but not so much on direction. I really am in the rat race.'

Pausing at that thought, Bob reminisces about the times he and his mother would enjoy their rent-controlled vacation on LBI. The owner of the property had frozen the price for 20 years, which was unheard of in those times — probably even more so now. But lots of people did amazing things for his mother, Kath. She was Bob's rock and to lose her so young shook him to his core. Perhaps it was this jolt that propelled him to run so fast with the other rats, when he could have taken time to consider a different race altogether.

Bob tells himself it is time to find more meaning and discover his real purpose. 'That's it', he thinks. 'I need a bigger purpose for my life — a personal purpose with meaning and deeper values, before it's all over in the blink of an eye.'

He already knows he wants to be deeply remembered by his family. This is not as an ego-driven wish; rather it is a desire to benefit their lives through a positive legacy. But there's something about his wider community too that he can't leave behind.

'What about work?' he thinks. His mind drifts as he looks up again at the lighthouse. Remembering it once had flames that were central to its purpose to help navigate and protect, he finds himself wondering about the optic prisms that direct the light. In between his panting and contemplation this analogy snaps him back to work.

'Our bank's purpose needs to be our central light! Our vision, strategy, values, principles and goals all need to shine, direct and reflect this single light from every angle', he thinks, his mind whirring.

Company values need to give the light depth and ardour, he knew. And everything and everyone needs to be infused with this light — this single unifying purpose with meaning. It is this light that will inspire everyone to commit and act.

'We don't do this at all', he thinks suddenly. 'Half of what we do is budget-directed. And the other half is for the capital markets, our shareholders.

'Our formal statements mention customers and, having worked my way up through the branch network, I like to think I have the customer front of mind. But when do I actually *meet* customers these days? I spend most of my time in internal meetings, steering groups and offsite conferences — or stuck under a pile of paperwork. Could it be that I only work to get my bonus?'

And so it happens. Bob has an epiphany, which comes as he stands at the foot of his favourite lighthouse: *change starts with me.*

'I look after almost 1000 people. I can create a lighthouse — a beacon — within the bank.'

Bob picks up a stick and writes *purpose* in the nearby sand. 'I get it', he thinks. He then draws a director's chair to represent setting the purpose in motion. He draws the chair on the letter P, as its pillar.

'I have to live on-purpose.'

Feeling buoyed by his drawing, Bob takes a photo on his phone before it gets washed away. A cool breeze across Bob's cheek reminds him dusk is settling and it's time to leave. With new strength in his stride, Bob runs home. He looks forward to a big sleep before the long drive home in the Sunday Jersey Shore traffic.

Bob pounds the pavement thinking he may just have had his second epiphany.

Week three, day one
PLOT comes to life

Travelling back in time to the start of the week, Ms Molloy has a spring in her step on this Monday morning.

She enjoyed planning PLOT last night and she is excited about her weekend discovery. But in spite of her brainwave, she still carries a heavy brick of dread in her stomach at the thought of completing and presenting her excursion paperwork to the principal. She knows the children will benefit from a trip to a real bank, but the paperwork undermines her enthusiasm.

Mrs Doogan is a stickler for detail—especially when it comes to anything that creates additional risk and liability. Never one to take chances, it is safe to say the conservative principal is very set in her ways.

Before their early morning meeting, Ms Molloy goes through the guidelines one last time, proving that a trip to the bank is educationally valuable. They outline the costs and the dreaded risk assessment. She has had to think of everything from bee stings to dogs to automatic sliding doors—oh, the tedium.

Ms Molloy tries to remember if there are any sliding doors at the branch that could possibly squash the children. 'The last thing I need is a sliding door moment', she thinks to herself.

* * *

The bell rings for the start of class and Ms Molloy snaps everyone to attention—there is a lot to cover today, now that the excursion plans have been approved by Mrs Doogan. Ms Molloy knows the class will go crazy over the excursion announcement, so she announces it like pulling off a bandage.

'Quickly and quietly please class, as I have an important announcement.' The class scrambles to attention; they know it is something important when Ms Molloy is abrupt.

'I have exciting news today. To help us understand what we have to *do* and what we *need* for our banks, we are going on an excursion.

'Yes, we are going to visit a bank!' Ms Molloy waits patiently so the children can have their moment, which, predictably, involves screams, shouts and lots of questions.

'Enough', she eventually says with enough force to calm the class in an instant. 'I will give you a permission slip to take home and I need it returned by the end of the week if you want to go. On Monday we will be walking to the Glen Fark County branch of Synergy Bank.'

Ms Molloy also needs parent helpers—although the word 'helper' is not always the best description. So often in the past, parents have shown up uninvited, asked silly questions and popped out mid-excursion to get coffee. Once a parent even sat in a corner texting on their phone all day! But with years of excursions behind her, Ms Molloy knows a savvy selection is the best way forward and so she quietly asks Betsy if her mother Vikki would like to come. Ms Molloy knows Vikki well—she always sends little gifts and thank-you cards. She is the kind of mother who takes the time to write absentee notes on nice paper. How she does this, Ms Molloy has no idea. A single mother who works fulltime in IT, Vikki still zooms in to volunteer her time and make it to every assembly. And it goes without saying that everyone just loves Betsy's behaviour.

Vikki often puts herself last so that her girls can have everything they would have had if their father had not left. And he left when Betsy was two, by the way, because he had an affair. But Vikki is not a woman to let divorce stop her from creating generational change in her family. 'A great asset to the excursion', thinks Ms Molloy, desperately hoping she will be able to come.

Next, Ms Molloy makes a note to invite Bobby's dad. He emailed her late last night to confirm his presentation date. Having him on the excursion would be a great opportunity to help the class understand his upcoming presentation!

Keen to settle the excursion uproar as quickly as possible, Ms Molloy heads straight into today's task. 'Betsy and Bobby, please get your groups together and sit in a circle with your whiteboards. We are going to create lists of all the jobs we think your banks are going to need to do. I also want you to think about what the banks will need—you know, Big Question 4. Things like paper, pens, computers, printers, ATMs … You have ten minutes to work on this.'

Ms Molloy sits down and grabs her folder full of her newly created PLOT worksheets in the shape of a four-leaf clover. After ten minutes, she invites her secret class favourites, Julia and Nicholas, to the front to hand them out.

'Class, I want your full attention. Now we all know our four Big Questions, and we've been thinking about each one individually. Now it's time to summarise them all into something that's very easy for you to remember so that you think of them *all at once.*

'What I have created is a special word made from the first letter of each our four Big Questions. Can anyone tell me the word that combines the first letters of a few words to create another word?'

A hand flies in the air. Surprise, surprise—it belongs to Julia. 'Excellent', Ms Molloy says once Julia announces the word 'acronym' loudly and confidently.

She writes their new acronym on the whiteboard with its four questions dotted around it.

Purpose **L**eadership **O**perations **T**echnology = PLOT

Then she asks the class to look at the worksheet so they can PLOT how to make a great bank. The advanced students like the acronym;

the creative students like the clover; and—well—almost everyone likes a good plot.

Ms Molloy turns to write some notes on the board and says, 'Please write down:

1 your bank's name at the top

2 your purpose in the P leaf

3 what you learned about how to behave in the L leaf, and

4 your to-do lists in the O and T leaves, ensuring anything that requires electricity is in T.'

After what seems like an eternity, the students finish their worksheets and it is time to remind them about the role their parents are playing in the assignment.

Ms Molloy recaps about the need for checkers—or regulators—and reminds the class that they are a group of people who make sure everyone is following the rules, and who help change the rules if necessary.

Then Ms Molloy asks Sally and Abby to come to the front of the classroom to hand out an update note for their parents.

RE: Your invitation to participate in this term's assignment to build a bank

Dear Parents,

As you know, we have been working hard on our exciting build-a-bank assignment this term and your child is about to head off on an excursion to the local Synergy branch. During the trip we want to gather as many observations as possible — but we also want every child to understand the basics of banking.

As you will know, risk is a big part of banking that is much too complex to cover in detail in this assignment.

Instead, we will focus on the need for governance and controls, appropriate incentives (our class metaphor for employee bonuses is our pre-approved candy jar) and the right culture (please see your child's four-leaf clover, which they will bring home today).

We would like you to review these in the context of your role as a parent, to bring some governance to this assignment.

We had a lesson on the purpose of regulators last week — and everyone understands that the role is very important. That's why we have asked you to be the regulators for your child's bank and have compiled a few questions we are hoping you will consider and answer.

1 How do you set rules for home? How do you reward good behaviour? How does this help the behaviour of everyone in the family?

   We believe that the context of home will be an excellent analogy for the leadership of their bank and help the children understand these concepts.

2 With this in mind, how do the bankers decide who to lend money to and how much to give them?

We believe that trust, faith and intuition play a big role in making these decisions. We would like your input, as we believe this thought-process that permeates life emanates from one's upbringing.

Please discuss these questions with your child. Thank you so much for participating in this assignment.

The curriculum this term is centred on the importance of good ethics and our humanity.

Regards,
Ms Molloy

PS. Please feel free to use any online resources to help with your answers. The workings of banks can often be a mystery to us all!

With the notes handed out, Ms Molloy awaits the recess bell and dreams of her next coffee fix.

'Quick reminder, everyone!' she calls as the children start to pack up their bags. 'Bring in your excursion notes tomorrow *and* work on your assignment at home with your parents. That means you need to give them the update note as well!'

It's not always easy to tell if a class of eight-year-old students is listening when they're rummaging in their bags and the bell is ringing for recess. But Ms Molloy will worry about that another day.

Week four, day one
The bank

The big day has finally arrived and the excitement is palpable. Vikki and Bob are on time and suited up so they can dash back to work afterwards. But they both seem focused on all the children from the start, which is more unusual than you might imagine. Despite going through the rigmarole of the Working with Children Check, some parent helpers quickly forget their responsibility for the children as a group and instead their gaze follows their own child. Sometimes they'll even hold hands with them and pass out snacks outside of break time!

Ms Molloy rings her hand-bell and looks around expectantly, but no-one moves.

'I think this bell is broken because no-one is listening to me!' she calls out dramatically. 'Or perhaps it's because no-one wants to go on the excursion after all!' At this, everyone dashes to their seats.

Completing the roll count is critical on days like today, so this is her priority. She gives the checklist to Vikki and Bob and says, as she always says, 'Leave no man behind'.

'Okay, everybody! Who can tell me why we are going to Synergy Bank?' she asks.

Eager to impress his dad, Bobby raises his hand and Ms Molloy chooses him. 'We are going to the bank so we can understand the *doing* parts—their operations and technology', he says, pointing to the PLOT worksheet on his clipboard.

'Fantastic, Bobby! Can someone else share why we are going?' Betsy puts her hand up. 'Of course', thinks Ms Molloy, who can do nothing but choose her.

'We are going to watch and listen. To see how the people who work at the bank behave and how happy the customers are', she answers, clutching her clipboard officiously to her chest.

'Great points, both of you. Anyone else, other than our leaders?'

David Hehman pipes up. 'I hope we get to play on the ATM machine! My parents never let me touch it.'

'That is for good reason, David. Money machines are not toys. Before we get going, we have a few things to go through. Betsy and Bobby, please make sure everyone is contributing equally to the PLOT worksheets, not just you. We are going to have question time when we get back so please all be prepared.

'Okay, time to pack up. Make sure you have your clipboard, your PLOT worksheet, your pencil and your buddy.

'Remember our excursion rules: know your parent leader. Today is a unique day because the parents of your leaders, Betsy and Bobby, have joined us, so they are your leaders too! Be polite, be courteous and listen. Now everyone go to the toilet and we will meet at the gate in five minutes.'

Ms Molloy is waiting at the gate, where she starts counting heads and pressing her clicker as they pass through the gate. She asks Vikki and Bob to also count heads for extra assurance, but as the leader she knows she still holds overall accountability—and she holds this in her heart.

'Okay, we are going to walk to the bank in lines of two: boy, girl. If you don't walk properly we are all going to hold hands!' Ms Molloy warns. 'That always works', she smiles conspiratorially to herself.

In Ms Molloy's risk assessment, she counted the roads to cross between the school and the bank—six—and shared this with the parents. She should also have shared that no matter how many times you tell a line of children to move quickly, no-one will move any faster. But the children never remember Ms Molloy telling them off the whole time they are on school excursions—they only remember the joy and adventure of learning outside of the classroom. And while Ms Molloy's overall purpose is education for the assignment, she also has an important mission to get back incident-free!

School banking is a big part of Synergy's retail strategy, so they have organised for their employee Steve to be at the branch, loaded up with piggybanks and information displayed on colourful sheets.

Steve is a man who loves his job, partly because he possesses that unique patience for the curiosity of children (up to the last school's excursion to his branch, at least). So as he shows the class around the branch he highlights the importance of a good computer system, knowing your customer, being nice, being safe, and having special areas for customers who need to talk to a banker. He gladly answers all questions from the children, however silly they might appear to adults.

'Yes we do meet lots of rich customers', he responds to one such question. 'But that doesn't always mean they have a lot of money.' He laughs gently as some of the kids screw up their eyebrows in confusion or protest loudly. 'You can be rich in many different ways—and it's a bank's job to remember that. That's why we value *all* of our customers, no matter how much money they have.'

Ms Molloy lets out a smile at this but at the same time she spies David Hehman edging back and forth in front of the sliding door sensor so it continually opens and closes. She swiftly walks over and tells David to stand away from the sensor. As he does so, he puts his finger behind the sliding door and ruins Ms Molloy's mission to avoid an incident.

'David, you had a good opportunity to make a decision—a right or wrong decision—just like our word "ethical"', she preaches, as David holds out his red, squashed finger in surprise. 'The right thing to do would have been to listen to me, but you chose to ignore me.

Now I will have to give your parents a call, as there have just been too many incidents. Please join the group now.'

Ms Molloy looks at the entrance and knows that life is full of sliding-door moments. She worries for these Hehman boys. She sees their potential but knows they have had many years without boundaries. Everyone needs to know where the line is or calamities are sure to occur.

Steve from Synergy concludes by handing out the piggybanks, which delights the children no end. And, oh yes, there is also one for Bob, Vikki and Ms Molloy! Their piggybanks are a little different, of course. They are stuffed with Steve's shiny business card. 'If there's anything you want to discuss', he says by way of explanation.

'We have a great deal on home insurance at the moment. It really does rival—'

'Thank you, Steve', Ms Molloy responds quickly. 'We really must get back. Come on class! Into your pairs!'

On the walk back to school, the children—revved up from having the opportunity to scrunch some real money in their hands, even though they had to give it back—insist on jumping on and off the curbs. Of course, someone has to trip and fall. 'Just my luck', thinks Ms Molloy, striding over to Sally to inspect the damage.

Back in the classroom, Ms Molloy settles the class and thinks again of the hot, bitter coffee that's waiting for her at recess. Looking around the room, she can tell that Vikki and Bob are over it too and are looking forward to going back to their respective jobs. But then all parents underestimate the energy it takes to manage an excursion.

Ms Molloy rings her class bell and asks Betsy and Bobby to come to the front of the room. She always gets her class to create Certificates of Appreciation to thank the parents who have helped. The parents love it and the exercise teaches the class gratitude. As Vikki and Bob receive their certificates, Bob glances down to read the scrawled words: 'Thank you for your time today. It means a lot to our class.' He has that funny sinking feeling again and he casts his mind back to last weekend at the Barnegat Lighthouse. But before he can get too nostalgic, he and Vikki are applauded out of the room by a classroom of children.

'Right class, now we are going to recap what we learned', Ms Molloy tells the room. 'We are going to start by reminding ourselves of the purpose of our banks, BBG and BoH. Then each team leader will talk about what they saw at Synergy Bank today, what they wrote down, and how this helps the bank do what it says it wants to do—its purpose.'

Betsy goes first, her piece of paper so full of notes that some sections are written sideways. 'I noticed that bankers and banks have a lot of things they need to do and there were a lot of computers and other things in the bank. We all tried to write everything down but ran out of space. We also think that maybe the people who work at the bank would not understand our purpose.'

'That's an interesting point, Betsy. Can you read your purpose again please?'

Betsy reads their purpose:

> BoH's purpose is to make customers happy by giving and taking money. Also to make their staff happy, as this is what will make customers happy.

'Did you mean that you don't think people will *remember* your purpose, Betsy?'

'No, Ms Molloy. We don't think they'll *understand* it because we are not sure if it will mean anything to them. They have so much to do and so many rules and the customers are all so different. We think it needs to be simpler.'

'I see. And did you come up with any ideas?' asks Ms Molloy.

'Yes', chirps Betsy. 'We thought the feelings were most important so we have decided to change our purpose.' Betsy holds up the new purpose written on the back of a PLOT worksheet while her group reads it out loud:

> BoH's purpose is to make customers happy by giving them what they need, to have the people in the bank be happy and nice to customers, and to make money.

'We think this one is easier for everyone to understand', she explains. And then, lowering her voice she adds, 'We also saw someone in the bank be a little mean to one of the customers. We think they were … frustrated. So we thought it best to make sure the word 'nice' was in our purpose.'

'Good thinking, Betsy's group! Is there anything else?'

'Yes, we think there is a lot of paper in the bank that doesn't have a purpose. We think it needs less paper.'

'Great observations! Now it's time for you Bobby.'

'We saw a lot of the things that Betsy's group saw, but we also saw loads and loads of different pictures all over the walls. They all had the same logos on them, so David said that our bank should have a cool logo just like his ice hockey team does!'

'We think our new purpose is so good!' he continues proudly, as David pretends to swing a hockey stick at Julia's head.

BBG's purpose is to make shareholders and customers happy.

The lunch bell rings as Ms Molloy thanks the class, quietly impressed with their observational skills. Then, with no more time to lose, she makes a beeline for her coffee.

Week four, day five

Bob's upcoming visit

The week has passed in a blur of lessons and paperwork and Ms Molloy needs to prepare and remind everyone of next week's guest visitor, Bob the banker! She hums the song to *Bob the Builder* in her head and chuckles inwardly.

'Just a quick reminder, everyone, that Bobby's dad, Mr Turner, will be sharing his banking experiences with us on Monday. Remember how we went to the bank this Monday? Well now the bank is coming to you! Please think of some good questions to ask him and remember they must relate to our assignment. No silly questions please.'

Ms Molloy just knows someone is going to ask if Bob has a fridge in his office, or something like that. It happens every time.

'Now off you go! Have a great weekend.'

'A good end to a long week', she thinks, as the classroom empties in seconds. She wonders, not for the first time, if anyone appreciates how hard she works.

Week five, day one

Bob's presentation

Bob wakes up very early, filled with trepidation. 'Ridiculous', he thinks, given the amount of public speaking he does. He wonders why he is so nervous. He reflects back to Barnegat Lighthouse and knows he cannot just present the standard corporate spiel, with the vision and mission statements and all that other stuff. He doesn't want to let Bobby down. He takes a swig of his wife's flower remedy to calm himself.

Ms Molloy arrives with the exact opposite mindset. She bumps into Mrs Laforte in the staffroom. 'I dropped Bobby's dad an email, but he was too busy to speak to me', she says, forgetting her purpose. 'I just wanted to brief him on what I would like him to cover ...'

Mrs Laforte has always had a lot of time for Ms Molloy. 'Just try to coach him if he gets off message. Did he read your email?'

'His secretary did but I am not convinced he's read it', snipes Ms Molloy. 'There goes the bell.'

Bob arrives and Ms Molloy spots the nerves. 'Bloody hell', she thinks. 'A nervous bank executive presenting to a bunch of eight-year-olds. Just what I need on a Monday.' Ms Molloy greets Bob cordially, checks he has read the email and is clear on the brief. Bob says he is on track, but Ms Molloy is not convinced.

The class settles quickly and Bobby is like a beacon of joy at his desk, making Ms Molloy extremely happy and reminding her to pull her own head in when emotions spill over.

Bob looks at the sea of expectant faces and starts rambling on about mission, vision, values and products, lots of buzz words — and on it goes. He's not sure why he's doing this. It is exactly what he *didn't* want to do.

Ms Molloy can see he is losing the class. She decides to start question time early and starts off by asking Bob one of her own.

'Bob, our assignment starts with the class having a purpose for the bank. The purpose defines their cause. Can you share what your bank's purpose is?'

There is a very long, uncomfortable pause. 'Bloody hell', thinks Ms Molloy. 'Really? Is this really happening?' Ms Molloy, like her mother, likes to say 'bloody hell' a lot. In her head, mostly.

Bob asks for a chair. He sits on it backwards and Ms Molly is reeling once more. She spends so much time on chair protocols! She decides to let it go... Oh no, now that song from *Frozen* is in her head...'Let it go' is now consuming her! This is becoming her worst nightmare.

Bob turns to speak only to Ms Molloy, aggravating her further. 'Well Ms Molloy, quite frankly I don't want to share our bank's purpose because I am not sure it is going to make any difference to your class's understanding of our bank, let alone *their* banks.

Our bank has too many confusing statements—purpose, visions, missions—and it is hard enough for the people who work for me to integrate and actualise them, let alone a bunch of eight-year-olds.'

Ms Molloy's momentary joy at seeing Bob open up is replaced by disappointment at the end of his speech. How does he think that makes her class feel?

'Really, what eight-year-old is going to have any clue what this guy is talking about?' she thinks to herself.

'Clearly he just did a corporate leadership course that popped in Maslow's hierarchy and now this guy is heading for a detour to an Indian ashram ...' she thinks, a little bitterly. 'I really don't need this. I just want the guy to do show-and-tell like a grown-up and let my class know that bankers care about customers. Am I expecting too much?' she asks herself.

Of course none of this comes out of her mouth. Instead Ms Molloy moves her head up and down slowly in a knowing, coaching way, egging Bob to get back on message.

Cue Bob, who pauses awkwardly to look down over the back of the chair. 'I have been doing a lot of thinking about my bank's purpose ever since Bobby asked me to participate in your assignment', he admits. The class is all ears. 'Whether by design or accident', he adds, glancing knowingly at Ms Molloy, 'I have become a student of your assignment'.

'It takes a lot of courage for me to say that in front of you kids, as I am supposed to be teaching you! What I am learning is that my bank's purpose is not big enough. You know your New Big Words and Big Questions—they have made me see that we need to get bigger, that *I* need to get bigger. Bigger than shareholders. Big with our customers. Big with the people who work for us. Our purpose needs to boldly define our cause.'

Bob pauses and you could hear a pin drop. This has certainly come out of left field, and the look on Ms Molloy's face is priceless. 'Who gives a shit about seating etiquette when this is happening?' thinks Ms Molloy. 'This is brilliant. A socially conscious awakening! Where was he in 2008?'

Bob takes a long, deep breath and continues. 'I am not sure I will be able to change the purpose for the entire bank, but what I can do is start with myself—take responsibility. I can start with the 1000 employees, 10 000 customers and 20 partnerships I am responsible for. I can redefine what is possible by using the bank's current purpose and doing exactly what you have done with BBG and BoH.' He gestures at their whiteboards. 'I am going to inject more meaning. Something that we can all believe in.'

'I am going to take all these things', he says, as he waves the vision, mission, strategy and values papers in the air, 'and connect them with our meaningful purpose!'

Bob walks over to the picture of PLOT and points to the last three letters: LOT. 'Kids, this is where the rubber hits the road. These three letters indicate where the work gets done. I am going to do my LOT to bring our new meaningful purpose alive in our bank.'

'You know kids, what we do matters', says Bob, now on a roll. 'What *each* of us does, every day, matters.

'I have come to realise that we are all leaders. Not just me, not just Bobby, not just Betsy, but all of us.

'Leaders come from anywhere, whether they manage a team of 1000 or they lead themselves through each day.'

Ms Molloy is in shock. She feels like she's in the front row of a TEDx talk, feeling like her mind is being downloaded into Bob's speech.

'So kids, I am leaving your classroom, now *my* classroom, to head into the city to start enabling change. But it starts with me. I need to change. I need to be a courageous leader. I need to let everyone *see* me.'

Bob stands up, moves the chair to one side and says with the look of a wide-eyed innocent child, in a much stronger New York accent than earlier, 'So kids, there's the PLOT to my new story.'

Ms Molloy is gobsmacked. The sound of Mr Aitkens' drone next door is the only noise around the room.

The children, meanwhile, love Bob's speech. The cynical part of Ms Molloy wonders if it is just because the speech was given from a backward-facing chair—a dream come true, especially for the little boys.

Or did they all actually take it in?

Bobby is not sure what to think and looks to his classmates for assurance. To his relief, they all start clapping. They think Bob the banker is crazy and they love him. Betsy wonders whether he could mentor her at the Bank of Humanity.

'Wow, what a day', thinks Ms Molloy. Never one to drink on a Monday, she decides to ditch the tea tonight and have a big fat red to help digest the day.

Reflections

At home, snuggled in her favourite corner of the couch with her large glass of Australian shiraz, Ms Molloy feels satisfied.

She had stayed the course to prove that socially conscious business can be taught in elementary schools, and that teachers play a pivotal role in society—and for that, Ms Molloy gives herself a big tick. A big mother of a TICK.

Week five, day two

Customers rule

Ms Molloy thinks it's wise to start the day with the most enormous coffee possible: she can only imagine the questions she will get from the class after yesterday's unexpected parental performance.

Ms Molloy chooses to get in front of the situation, as always, and decides the best approach is to quickly find a leadership lesson out of Bob's speech. She considers the myriad possibilities. Bob's public outburst about his bank's weak purpose highlights the importance of being open to change, but most importantly it demonstrates the importance of being courageous. Without courage it is hard to invite change in. Without courage it is hard to believe things are possible. Bob showed courage yesterday. He could have sauntered in as the big-kahuna banking executive but instead he turned his chair around—eventually the right way—and revealed himself to the class. 'Perfect', thinks Ms Molloy. 'Let's focus on courage and change.'

Ms Molloy knows all too well that change is the new normal. From the state government, the federal government, the district ... Oh, the politics and their impact on her school, it never stops.

To start, Ms Molloy decides to highlight and celebrate the work of both groups in calibrating their purpose during the course of the assignment. They knew they needed to change and showed great optimistic attitudes so they could make the change happen.

'Class I would like to start by congratulating all of you. You are doing such a good job in creating your banks—you decided, without help from me, to change your bank's purpose as you learned more throughout the course of the assignment. You had the courage to speak up. You had the courage to change. You should be very proud. As we heard from Bobby's dad yesterday, sometimes adults need to see life through the eyes of a child. You were Bob's teacher yesterday!' There are proud smiles all around.

Ms Molloy knows that with today's escalating narcissism and its 'me, me, me' culture, it is time to focus on the customer. Her class has spoken about the customer a lot but she is not convinced that they really understand what this means. How do you have a customer-focused mindset in a world that's drowning in a self-centred culture?

Thinking on her feet, she glances to her bookshelf and spots her favourite books by Dr Seuss—her life lessons hero author. She grabs *Horton Hears a Who* and decides to read it to the class. Dr Seuss nails it every time—Horton and his cohort learn that everyone's important, no matter how small they are. If only organisations in the real world showed such comprehension!

The class knows to expect question time after reading, so Julia sits up in anticipation. Ms Molloy summarises while slowly closing the book. 'So we can take from this book the same message we got from Steve at the bank: let's make sure that all of our customers matter to us!'

'Since both groups have rewritten their purposes to include the customer I thought it would be fun to imagine all the different types of customers; as the story teaches us, we need to make sure we hear the voices of all our customers.

'So close your eyes and imagine all your customers. How would you know what they want, what they need?'

It was great to see Abby's hand go up after a time, and Ms Molloy pounces on the opportunity before anyone else can offer an answer. 'We would just listen to everyone, no matter how much money they had?' offers Abby.

'Out of the mouth of babes', Ms Molloy thinks. Replacing her thoughts quickly, she says, 'Exactly Abby. It is that simple.

'With this understanding, I want you to get back into your groups and come up with ideas on how you would listen to your customers to help make your operations and technology—the things you do and the things you need, your *how*—work better to create happy customers', she says.

'By listening you can create new ideas that could make your bank the greatest bank in the world! Keep going until the bell rings.'

Julia is beside herself and lets out an excited gasp as she runs over to claim the coloured markers.

Week six, day one
Back to Bob

Meanwhile, Bob is starting to wonder if he is having a midlife crisis. Last he checked he wasn't cheating on his wife and hadn't bought a sports car, so what was going on?

Could he be experiencing a crisis of conscience?

Between his moment at the lighthouse and his weird presentation to the class last week, Bob needs to get this shit straight in his head.

So he does what he always does when faced with a problem: he puts on his running shoes and hits the pavement. Nothing like a good, long run to clear the head.

As sweat gathers on his brow, Bob realises that he needs to look within himself before he can rock up at the bank and give any kind of monumental keynote speech to change the world. *He* needs to change.

He realises that the rat race has been slowly stripping away pieces of him, over a long period of time. It is the kind of loss that you don't notice until it is too late. The grind of the day to day, the pressure to fit in, the budget challenges, the endless managing up … it is sucking the life out of him.

The lure of the bonus has left him barren.

Bob recalls a sentiment from Henry David Thoreau that he has never previously grasped — and, quite aptly, his brain replaces the original word 'men' with 'people': 'Many people go fishing all of their lives without knowing it is not fish they are after.'

Bob thinks back to the lighthouse and decides the solution is quite simple.

'I will re-evaluate my personal values and get a bigger purpose with more meaning than simply being a great family guy who has "made it".'

Bob knows this could take some time, as he wants to get it right. He's not getting any younger, after all. In ten years Bobby will be all grown up. He does not want to be the guy in *that* Harry Chapin song, an unreliable stranger to his son.

Now back home and desperate to clear his head of the noise, Bob glances at the fridge and thinks some cool beers will help. As he grabs the door, he gets glitter all over his hand and sees *those* words again—'humanity' and 'ethical'. Boom. That's it.

Bob takes a long, considered sip of his beer and knows what he has to do. He thinks, 'I need to bring my humanity to work every day'. He needs to *reveal* himself honestly to his customers, his team, his management and his suppliers. To *be* real—live real—be open and committed.

He realises his mind is echoing the excited hype that he's used to hearing from Brené Brown and Oprah (before he switches the channel). Could they be right? Is the key really to reveal your true, authentic and vulnerable self?

Bob leans back on the fridge and thinks about the insight trip that the executive team took to Silicon Valley last year. They were introduced to the concept of #flearn: learning through failure. At the time Bob thought this was just another buzzword from the Valley. But now he wonders if there is more to it than a satirical hashtag.

Certain that #flearn is not part of his psyche, let alone part of the culture of the bank, Bob resolves it's time to highlight his own failures publicly and openly discuss the learnings. It's a bold idea when everyone around him hides their mistakes. Cover-up is common.

Bob swigs his beer and thinks back to the GFC. Insufficient reforms, debt-fuelled consumption, fraud-fuelled booms, bad underwriting, short-term schemes, banks securitising: his stomach feels heavy with it all. Then a wave of nostalgia washes over him. 'Whatever happened to the banker who knew their customer, served the public purpose, and was in there for the long haul?' he wonders.

'I need to be that man. I need to reset my personal purpose for the good of more than just my family before I can lead any change at work.'

Bob starts imagining what this could look like at work.

Week six, day five

TGIF

'TGIF', thinks Ms Molloy as she drags herself to school. 'One quick lesson and then an easy day of art and music.'

'Quiet please', she says sharply, exhausted and ready for the weekend. 'Next Monday your groups are going to present the assignment— your bank. We are going to go over the marking scheme, you know, the rubric I gave you at the start of the assignment. This is because we need to measure the success of your banks against these criteria, otherwise we have failed to meaningfully capture this positive change', she says.

The class love having their work marked to defined criteria, believe it or not. They like a clear winner!

'Only one team can win and I want everyone to participate. I expect everyone to use PowerPoint. Your slides should include your bank's name and you can include a picture or a logo if you like. By 'logo' I mean something like this', she says, pointing to her empty coffee cup.

'Remember to include your purpose, why it is meaningful, how you need to behave as a leader, what you need to do, your operations, and what you need to have, your technology.

'I recommend using your PLOT sheet—also known as our clover—to help structure your presentation. Keep answering the simple questions of *why* and *how* whenever you get stuck.'

She hands out a sheet with everything she just said on it.

'Any questions?' she asks. 'Yes Betsy?'

'Ms Molloy, can we get our parents to help since they are our checkers, I mean regulators?'

'A fair question, Betsy.' Ms Molloy smiles, reflecting on how many parents had told her they'd enjoyed being involved in such a meaningful project—that hadn't involved multiple tools from their precarious sheds. 'Once complete, you may ask them to check your work and see if anything needs to be adjusted if it is too risky for a bank.

'Anyone else?' No-one speaks. 'Fantastic', thinks Ms Molloy.

Week seven, day one

Presentations

It is a cracker of an autumn day—cool and crisp with not a cloud in the sky, and brightly coloured leaves dancing in the breeze. Ms Molloy springs out of bed, gets her new Zara outfit out of the wardrobe and pairs it with her loop scarf, feeling pretty fabulous. She has a fantastic sense of style, which the girls in her class adore—it's always a talking point!

Art, computer and even music lessons have all been designed around the assignment this week. The excitement in the air is palpable; the kids love the creativity involved in building a bank and are hopefully learning that building any organisation can be a very creative pursuit. 'Creativity is the next greatest commodity in business', thinks Ms Molloy.

Creating the logos for the banks is a very popular aspect of the assignment, but Ms Molloy cannot believe some of the ideas coming through. They are straight off the front of a DVD cover. She had always felt that the influence of pop culture could drain people's creativity, and she decided it was time for an intervention. At that, Ms Molloy banned everything and anything related to game heroes or cartoons.

For most of the students, presenting is the most difficult thing they will do all year. It is clear how nervous some of the children are, and Ms Molloy is sympathetic: she knows how nervous she feels in front of the principal.

To help the class, Ms Molloy has suggested a very simple format. Each group is asked to restate the bank's purpose on the first slide, show their logo on the second, and then on slides three, four and five demonstrate the way they will use leadership, operations and technology to perform their purpose. Each message should have three key points. Everyone in the class gets a chance to speak.

As presentation time rolls around, Ms Molloy selects names out of a hat to decide who will go first. She decides it is the only possible democratic approach in keeping with the values of this assignment, which has grown so much bigger than she had anticipated.

When Bobby's name is drawn, he is asked to decide whether his group would like to go first or last. He decides to go first. Ms Molloy is not surprised.

Bobby's presentation

Bobby and his group come to the front of the room, all standing quietly and to attention. 'So cute', Ms Molloy thinks with pride.

They stand in horseshoe formation holding their palm cards in their hands and look like a united team. Ms Molloy is excited. They really did learn that New Big Word 'collaborate' quickly.

It's a tricky concept to teach, she knows. But, as she sees it, the open-source world we live in inspires us to collaborate. The new world order has yet to hit the curriculum, but that is not stopping Ms Molloy—the entrepreneur of the public school system!

In keeping with the structure, Bobby and his team present their slides and use the notes that they memorised for their speech.

Purpose

BBG's purpose is to make shareholders and customers happy.

Logo

'We thought the name of the bank was the most important part of the logo so we made it big and we included the big bull from Wall Street so the shareholders would be happy.'

Leadership — some of the ways we need to *be*

1 Strong
2 Brave
3 Happy

Operations — what we need to *do*

1 Fix what is broken

'When the group was at Synergy Bank we noticed that things were broken. We know because we heard customers saying things like 'you need to fix that', 'that is not what I was told on the phone'. By honestly saying what is broken and fixing it, it really shows how brave we are.'

2 Throw away the candy

'We really like thinking about cool stuff for BBG and we don't need lots of candy to do that. Well, we would like a *little* bit of candy but it's not going to help us create big ideas. This is also because my dad said that candy seems to create a lot of problems — someone always feels a bit sick if they have too much.'

3 Make sure that all the people who work for BBG have what they need to do their job

'When we were at Synergy Bank, we heard customers asking the tellers questions but they always said "I'll have to ask my manager", or "I'm sorry I am not authorised to do that — you'll have to ring 1800synbank". We think that if everyone at BBG knew more it would make them feel smart and happy. And we think that would make the customers happy too.'

Technology—what we will *need*

1   Toys for customers!

'This was our favourite part! We would make sure everyone can play on the Xbox while they are waiting, and we would have Skylander playing on screens so people never got bored in the queue!'

2   Make an app

'We would make an app for our parents' phones that made banking like a game. It would feature a superhero called Bob the Banker who gets people everything they need and helps people who start losing, especially if they are losing money. It would be really cool if BBG could do that.'

3   Achievement boards

'Our team would like to have Achievements, like in Minecraft. We would like our bank to guide us and give us challenges to complete. We think this would help our customers get what they need and want.'

Ms Molloy is stunned. What an insightful presentation that keeps the customers at its heart! With a tickle in her throat, she starts to ask everyone in the class to give Bobby's team a round of applause, but the sound of claps and whoops is already ringing around the room as Bobby and his group take a bow.

Betsy's presentation

Next up, Betsy's group presents the Bank of Humanity, BoH. They walk up as a group and announce to Ms Molloy that they felt PowerPoint did not help to show how they were feeling. Julia pipes up to say that when she was at church, they used this cool presentation called Prezi where things floated in and out. They think this would help them show how they were feeling, which is important when you have purpose.

Ms Molloy smiles, loving the high achiever in Julia while at the same time feeling a bit frustrated that they didn't ask before changing the rules. 'How hypocritical', she thinks, chiding herself. 'Just a minute ago I was celebrating BBG's concept of autonomy. No-one ever said control and growth are easy to balance as a teacher!'

Looking up at the Prezi, the logo melts Ms Molloy's heart.

Purpose

BoH's purpose is to make customers happy by giving them what they need, to have the people in the bank be happy and nice to customers, and to make money.

Logo

'Lots of people caring for each other—showing a community but also one that makes money.'

Leadership—some of the ways we need to *be*

1 Good listeners

'So we can hear the voice of all our customers, Ms Molloy, like you taught us through Dr Seuss.'

2 Creative

'We think that the happiest people are those who get to be who they are, like the way you let us do things in class in our own special way. You ask us questions and how we came up with the answers. You make us feel special and we think our big ideas, like your Big Words and Big Questions, are able to be created and come true. We think both our customers and the people who work for BoH will want to be creative with their money.'

3 Ethical and humane

'Of course we need these, because they are our New Big Words. Isn't that the point Ms Molloy?'

Operations—what we need to *do*

1 Concierge

'Well, you see, Sally got to go to a hotel for high tea in New York City with her Great-Aunt Sissy and when they walked in a man in a very fancy suit helped them to where they needed to be. This would be a wonderful person to have in a branch, as everyone always needs something different and waiting in the wrong line can really make our parents cranky.'

2 Make things easy

'We think there should be no more paperwork. It's very easy to use computers to get to know customers. And we know almost all the customers feel comfortable using computers! And if not, we know it is easy to help them.'

3 Get your money anywhere for free

'Our parents always use their phones and they are always very upset if they forget to take their wallet out with them. We think you should be able to get money out through your phone if you need to!'

Technology — what we will *need*

1 Clean money

'We think the green paper gets very dirty and thought maybe if money was made of plastic it would be nicer and would make customers happy, especially if it did not rip.'

2 You get warnings or strikes on your phone

'We think there needs to be something that stops customers getting into trouble. You know, like when you parents see how much money they spent on their credit card? BoH would send a message like my mother's phone app that lets her know when she is eating too much.'

3 A real game!

'BoH will have a virtual world game that we all get to play in. We create the world we want and then BoH sends us a banker who makes it all become real!'

Ms Molloy is utterly astounded by this year's results! Assignments where the children participate and collaborate well together can feel like a double-edged sword to Ms Molloy. On the one hand, she loves seeing the students work as a team. On the other, she dreads the marking. That is one of the reasons she makes the criteria so very clear at the start—and what a difference she has seen in the quality of work when she has taken the time to define and communicate clear criteria!

She also knows that in real life (most of the time, at least) there is always a winner, and everyone needs to learn how to win and lose with grace. As tempting as it is to let both groups win—due to the exceptional quality of both assignments—Ms Molloy knows it would not be fair.

The marking criteria are simple. Each slide gets either a tick or a cross, and the greatest number of ticks wins. There is always subjectivity in these types of assignments, and often the teacher knows prior to the final presentation who is most likely to win, so it can be hard to contain what sounds like a bias!

But the bottom line is that the teacher has the final say, the final judgement. Remarkably, the students tend to manage the outcome well—give or take some tears. The result is always explicitly communicated on the back of a motivational speech.

Afterwards, Ms Molloy knows she will be inundated with questions: 'Please show me why!' and 'Please show me how!' But she never gets annoyed. Quite the opposite. She thinks it is wonderful! They are key questions for growth and development and Ms Molloy often wishes her interactions with losing adults were similar.

Ms Molloy tallies up her ticks and crosses to announce the winners. There were many lessons to be learned through this assignment, but for Ms Molloy the one factor underlying the overall quality of each assignment was the naming of the banks. The Big Bubblegum

Bank spoke to the idea that bigger is better, and its reference to a banned substance encouraged subversive behaviour that should have been changed—either by the group itself or by the parents.

The Bank of Humanity, on the other hand, sums things up perfectly in a world where the right brain is as important as the left—'and the intersection of the two will be our saviour', thinks Ms Molloy. The Bank of Humanity and its beautiful logo stands tall. This is the group's tipping point. She wonders if this outcome had anything to do with her little sneaky experiment of loading up Betsy's team with girls as the majority in the group. She can hear the naysayers in her head: subjective, coincidence, red herring…

Ms Molloy asked the class to sit in a circle so she could go through the results. With care, she announces Betsy's team as the winners but even as she says the words she can't help but ask herself, 'Who is the real winner in all of this?'

The answer, of course, is Bob.

She thinks of the famous saying 'Give me a child until they are seven, and I will give you the man'—or 'woman', Ms Molloy is quick to correct in her head. She concludes by treating herself with her own motivational speech: 'I like to think this assignment has helped to set these children up for their adult lives, at least in some way where humanity is at the heart of business.

'And as Bob has taught us all, you're never too old—or too big—to learn a better way of doing things.'

Ten years on

It is hard to believe ten years have passed. The students from Ms Molloy's class are now 18 years old and about to embark on their own purposeful lives.

Ms Molloy   Mrs Laforte   Mrs Doogan   Vikki   Steve

Bob   Bobby   Nicholas   Abby   Sally

Julia   Betsy   David & Johnny Hehman   Mr Hehman

Betsy is heading off to a renowned college in Connecticut to become a teacher. Her experiences throughout her schooling, particularly the lessons of Ms Molloy, have lit a flame in her to educate and lead—something she knows will help to make a difference. Betsy is an advocate for those who are marginalised, helping children from single-parent families get the same fair chance in life. Betsy shares the impact of her Grade 3 banking assignment often when mentoring, and points out how the game of Choice is your opportunity. Betsy is now calling herself Liz, which she prefers.

Bobby achieved average results in sport, academics and looks, but nobody sees Bobby as average. He is anything but average. Bobby is *that* guy! The guy every girl wants to talk to. The guy parents hope their daughters will marry. The guy who is accepted into any friendship circle, without judgement. He holds true to his core values in friendships, which accentuates his warm smile and unassuming stance.

Bobby has an impressive teen following online, largely because people connect with him and what he has to share. His original carefree posts were there purely to provide a source of humour. Soon he used this influence to create a community that is focused on the greater good (some may say on ethics, collaboration and humanity). He creates conversations online through his beautiful photography and profound captions that touch the hearts of his generation. Many people have told Bobby that he will be a great leader one day, but he already knows that everyone is a leader.

Nicholas has excelled in both sport and academics. He has two scholarship opportunities for Ivy League universities and is thinking Princeton will be his choice. He would like to stay close to his family and his girlfriend, and he has become quite fond of volunteering at the local charity he helps out on weekends. He sees it as a very promising pathway for future leaders to make change.

Julia was the Glen Fark prom queen and graduated in the top 1 per cent of her class. She will be studying at New York University,

NYC. On her orientation day she met a wonderful Italian boy named Gene and she dreams of long nights talking with him about literature and, one day, marriage. In the meantime, though, she is an intern for a publicity agency and is very excited about the idea of flying around in private jets—albeit while holding coffee—and sauntering into VIP areas with a borrowed press badge. Julia has chosen this career path hoping she will be able to raise large-scale awareness for any issues pertinent to her core purpose, while, of course, multitasking the bright lights that fill her dreams.

Sally has moved to Australia to study. They always said she was a bit different. Everyone knew that kid couldn't sit still, but who would have imagined she would travel so far to go to university Down Under? Smarter than her classmates ever realised, Sally is studying to be a biomedical engineer in Melbourne. She finds it hard to get her class to keep quiet in her tutorials. It seems there is a 'swivel neck' in every class the world over.

Abby has an amazing gift of listening, watching trends on social media and synthesising this into contemporary art that speaks to people on a deep personal level. Abby knows that raw humanity is the biggest contributor to viral content and suspects this is why her irreverent approach, with ethics at its core, has taken off in such a meaningful way across the globe. Quiet at eight, out there at 18!

Johnny and David Hehman's dad was arrested and is in jail now for further fraudulent actions. He is a public villain and is trending on Twitter. People often quip he should have been locked up ten years ago.

Johnny Hehman is in rehab and trying to work through his addictions. The therapy is going well. He's realising that every child starts out with the best intentions; he now needs to turn them into his choices.

David Hehman has discovered meditation and yoga, which are leading him to his greater purpose, and he is planning to spend time in an Indian ashram next year. The time away from the public eye is a relief for David. He is working hard on himself, as he does not want to hit the same slippery slope that Johnny is now trying to escape.

Mrs Laforte has retired and is spending her free time with her grandchildren, whom she adores. She is an incredible grandmother because she is an incredible teacher and mother.

Mrs Doogan moves between New Jersey, Barbados and London. Her summers are spent in Barbados with her husband, living on a lean budget. She wakes every morning thanking God for this day and sings out 'Morning!' to those passing by on her daily walks. Officially retired from her reputation as the rigid GFC Elementary principal, she is now reverently known as Aunty Janet to many.

Ms Molloy has been offered the role of Principal many times over the past ten years but she continuously turns it down. While many people assume that the leader is always at the top—that the principal has all the power and influence—Ms Molloy knows the difference that can be made on the ground, in the classroom, student by student.

Knowing that innovation is often at the edge, Ms Molloy has connected inspiring teachers all over the world. She also connects classrooms everywhere—particularly in developing countries—through a pioneering virtual mentoring and coaching program, which now has a global portfolio of over 100 mentees. Her most treasured moments are when she connects into the classrooms of rural India. Women there are pioneering micro classrooms, much like microfinance ten years earlier.

Ms Molloy met the man of her dreams in a whirlwind romance during one of her insight trips to India.

Ms Molloy is now expecting her second child and knows all the challenges of being a mother. She is regularly featured as a transformational leader in public education conferences, foremost in both America and Ireland, although the fire is catching fast.

Bob, our beloved banker, is CEO of his bank, which he has rebranded as the Bank of Humanity. It's Bob's way of acknowledging what he learned from Ms Molloy and her wide-eyed students.

Around the time of BoH's launch, Bob gave a TED talk that rocked the world. It all started when he took Ms Molloy's PLOT model and brought it to life (without the glitter) in the 12 weeks following that run on Long Beach Island. Bob has created unique programs in partnership with all types of organisations to redefine profit as meeting a purpose that includes social returns. Bob is a case study for transformational leadership.

Bob says the moral of his story for the past ten years has been to live life on-purpose, to be the leader of his life, and to bring his humanity with him everywhere he goes.

Steve could not change with the digitisation of everything at Synergy Bank and elected to retire early. As he says jokingly, the disruption disrupted him!

Vikki spent eight years working in the banking and finance industry, following on from her experience of Ms Molloy's class. Vikki has helped local businesses and young employees realise their dreams, and she went on to write a book. Vikki is now travelling the world and has remarried after meeting the love of her life on holiday in New Zealand (where men are men and … sheep are sheep). Vikki spends her time travelling between New York, Sydney and New Zealand, working to create on-purpose leaders and to solve our seemingly intractable environmental issues.

Epilogue

Hello, this is your author, known to my mates as KJ. I was planning on writing all about the future of banking, Banking 10.0, and all of the amazing client-centric, socially responsible innovation and disruptive technology that goes with it, but that would be ridiculous. (Who can predict anything in our seemingly unpredictable world?)

What I *can* share is some insight into Bob's character. Bob lives with purpose infused into his life. Bob realised his purpose by using his lighthouse metaphor to communicate the Bank of Humanity's purpose, its light source, so that every employee and customer became connected and committed in their own personal way. Known worldwide as a progressive leader, Bob's character is contagious, causing those around him to transform.

Bob's core values—courage, ethics and humanity—are the contagion, creating fellowship founded on shared commitment to the cause.

Bob knows not to fear the crowd but to wrap his arms around it. He knows not to fear the scientists but to listen carefully. Bob has replaced corporate fear with corporate curiosity. Bob knows that in order to lead he needs to live his personal and corporate purpose every day, as exhausting as it may be. Uncertainty is Bob's normal. He is steady and stays the course.

Bob doesn't have 'employees' and they are not the means to an end; Bob has a tribe of people who he stands beside, behind and in front of. He is a leader, a follower and a colleague. Bob has a steel wire connecting his head to his heart and he brings his humanity to work every day, ethically, no matter what the cost. Bob is also quite a funny guy and makes sure laughter is used as meaningful medicine.

Bob has spent the last decade taking great personal risk.

Who knows what banks will look like in a decade, or even if they will still exist? What we do know is that Bob will be brilliant and will PLOT success wherever he goes, whatever he does. Why? Because Bob is living life on-purpose.

Bob is our fable's hero even though I *really* wanted it to be Betsy. Interesting how you never can predict the ending, even when you are writing the story.

PART II
Manifesto

This book has been written on purpose — in the literal sense — as we head into a time when our models are failing to predict the future (of anything, from the weather to the economy). In the words of Winston Churchill, 'It's useful to look to the future but not further than you can see'. The majority of people accept that we have unprecedented change ahead and seemingly intractable issues to address; so how do individuals, government, corporates and not-for-profits steer their course? I love serendipity as much as the next guy, but it is not going to stop this ship from hitting the rocks.

What should be our rudder? How will we get there? What moral code do we hold on to without rationalising away what truly matters?

Why? Because it is hard to make everyone happy. It is hard to look after all our constituents — our family and friends, our customers, our employees, our community, our mother earth, our shareholders, our bottom line — ourselves. It is easy for one to dominate, one person, one interest group. Could we become the narcissist or simply forget to look after ourselves?

In the thick of this it is easy to rationalise a new truth. It is easy to make mistakes. It is easy for the wrong person to be leading.

In a world where so much is happening I look to one of our most brilliant minds, Albert Einstein, who said, 'Out of clutter, find simplicity. From discord, find harmony. In the middle of difficulty lies opportunity.'

I believe in simplicity, harmony and opportunity. I am an optimist.

This book's central thesis is that there must be a meaningful purpose at the core of our lives and our organisations. A purpose that all of our constituents — including ourselves — can find meaning in, that reflects the character of our being, that we can use to inform our decisions and our modes of operating, and build a community with — a construct for genuine harmony.

Weaving purpose through the core of what and how we get stuff done brings it to life. It moves things from platitudes to reality and manifests opportunity.

What's with the story?

'Back to School' is a fable. Fables are stories not founded in fact, typically featuring animals or inanimate objects as characters. This fable actually does have an animal character—you just can't see it. It is the elephant in the room. The elephant in the room is the underlying theme of the global financial crisis (GFC).

Many of the lessons we learned from the GFC are woven into the fable. The world's banking and finance organisations have already applied some of these, but there are still others that remain in the wings for a teacher to take on, waiting for the bell of another GFC to ring.

Perhaps in the distant future our children's children will see the GFC like a fable. Just like any good narrative they will see the complication, the resolution, the lessons learned and the moral. Perhaps by then all the lessons learned will have been attended to and the moral will have been widely applied.

So yes, I believe 'Back to School' is in fact a modern-day fable—with an elephant, bears (if you count the stock market), and hopefully morals. The fable illustrates how purpose can become the concentrated, high-intensity beam of light in your lighthouse: a light that can help you navigate through waves and around obstacles, no matter what lens you are looking through. Your lenses are important—they should be magnifying your light, not dimming it. Without our light we stray off course; some people hit the rocks, some get lost, and some sink. Sinking ships, as we know, are often irrecoverable.

We're so used to thinking that one pill can make us better that we often believe that everything is recoverable. But it isn't. Animals become extinct, rainforests disappear, corporations fail and people—well, we all know someone who has fallen off the rails. Sometimes, as we say, shit happens—and there is no way back.

So purpose is important. It helps us hold our course, it keeps us steady, it lights our way through rough waters.

This may sound very personal, and that's because it is. Organisations are personal. As a matter of fact, they are full of people. People fade or flourish. And life is no longer linear: it's a very squiggly line. Every desirable business plots their key measures and looks for the strong, straight trend line—hoping those scatter plot points don't squiggle too far from the trend.

Your purpose is your strong central trend line, your constant, driving straight through our squiggly, scatter-plot world.

The power of our story

In *our* story, the lighthouse was chosen for many reasons as the metaphor for Bob's awakening to the importance of purpose. Many people love lighthouses—as much for their beauty, architecture, history and engineering as for the stories told about them over the years. You know, the selfless lighthouse keepers who staffed the stations in isolation—all on-purpose: for the safety of others. Without the story of the keeper, would the romance of the lighthouse have endured?

Our minds are story processors, not logic processors—we retain more from a story.

Our story features Ms Molloy, who is its only real-life character. She is in real life an amazing teacher. Some characters in the fable are completely fictitious, while others have slivers and pieces from my life, which have been sprinkled in for fun, colour and a bit of personal cathartic release.

Stories, like life, don't always go the way you might expect. My original plan set up Betsy as the hero. The smart young girl rising to the top of the class wet my feminist whistle no end—and then the story unfolded. The moral of the story had to hail Bob, the hardworking executive with good intentions and misguided purpose, as the main protagonist.

In the fable, Ms Molloy leads the class through a wonderful term of creative thinking and self-discovery. She wants to press home the importance of having a clear, meaningful purpose backed by the right behaviours and actions — oh, and to have the students learn a bit of banking and finance along the way.

While Ms Molloy's class is full of potential, by the age of eight some children have unfortunately already experienced the impact of nurture over nature, and this class is no exception.

Ten years on it is clear that things have not ended perfectly. To have ended perfectly it would have to have been a fairy tale, and we all know there are no such things as fairy tales! (I know this all too well. I am still waiting for that knight in shining armour to show up. Where is that guy?)

I am talking about Johnny Hehman. Johnny turned left at that sliding door too many times. There are so many influences trying to persuade us to lean left instead of right, yet somehow, luckily, the majority of us turn right. But our Johnny didn't. I hope he finds his way. Would purpose help? I think so. Is it the panacea? I would love to believe that, but there are too many variables to even begin to make such a bold claim.

What I do know is that I come from a family where someone took a hard left. Not a day goes by where I don't think about that. I can't tell another person's story but I can tell my own. What's the difference in my family between the hard left and the right path? Three things: a bit of dysfunction, an affair, and a death — all followed by hard lefts.

The story is a modern-day tragedy and for another book. The point is — they got off-purpose and, with absolutely no pun intended, they lost the plot.

The point of sharing this isn't to air my family history. It's to share that I have seen what happens when someone goes off course. Whether consciously or subconsciously, this experience is a large part of my motivation to help people stay on course — to stay true and practically aligned to what is meaningful in their lives, to stay on-purpose — and is based on my experience of what happens when purpose is lost.

A bit about Ms Molloy

Ms Bolinda Molloy is my beloved *tidda* (an Aboriginal term for a woman who is like a sister...as well as a fantastic book called *Tiddas*, by Dr Anita Heiss). I have known Bolinda for 16 years. I met her as a traveller in Australia—Irish born, raised in England. Ms Molloy, known to her friends as Bo, is a primary school teacher. The way our Ms Molloy teaches in Glen Fark County, New Jersey (my state of origin), is how Ms Molloy now teaches in Sydney, Australia. A little poetic licence was used to merge my history with Bo's story with 'Back to School', our fable.

During our research together I went to her apartment and after unbolting her two locks—yes, she has a touch of OCD—she let me in! The moment I walked in, I saw a beautiful framed collage of 23 young students between the ages of seven and eight each holding a small blackboard with a single handwritten word on it. The collage was Bo's Christmas present from her wonderfully diverse class. Each child was asked to write one word that they thought best described Bo. Their blackboards read: brilliant, helpful, wonderful, incredible, tall, awesome, funny, cool, fantastic, lovely, wonderful, nice, graceful, kind, pretty, special, super, great, amazing, #1, creative, smart, and polite. The accompanying card was equally full of accolades.

Teachers make a massive difference by deriving purpose and meaning each day in their classroom. Every answer to that ever-asked question—'Why do we have to do this?'—presents a new purpose-rich opportunity. Teachers—like parents, bosses and leaders—have impact, be it good, bad or indifferent. How they behave matters. How they operate matters.

We need more teachers like Bo.

We need more people like Bo.

Most importantly we need more *leaders* like Bo.

Bo models her teaching style around the *why*, not because she has read Simon Sinek's latest book, but because this is the natural state of a child's mind. The inquisitive child, supported by a purpose-driven teacher, is free to be their creative, unique self. Bo knows that in kindergarten a child's capacity for creativity, their divergent thinking (aka Edward de Bono's 'lateral thinking') is at 98 per cent of a creative genius rating. Unfortunately, according to a longitudinal study described by George Land and Beth Jarman in their book *Breakpoint and Beyond*, children's creativity drops alarmingly and exponentially as they age. So in an attempt to keep everyone from falling off the creativity cliff, Bo fosters an enabling environment for *everyone*. From the dancers to the designers to the dentists and the disruptors, Bo is making and creating space for everybody. She believes that enabling creativity is as important as literacy. Her classroom makes room for every student. The *why* is not a dictatorship; it is directional question both *for* the children and *from* the children.

A bit about Bob

Bob, our unlikely protagonist, considers himself a likely leader. He did all the right things to get where he is in his career. But he really is a bit lost, unknowingly of course, until he too becomes Ms Molloy's student. He lives in a world where everything is becoming open and transparent, yet he works in a traditional 'corporate' world where hierarchy and confidentiality reign (unless, of course, 'management decide to share'). His office is surrounded by images of people working on laptops beside a blissful clean river, and yet he is hauling it in every day on the train—except for his 'flexible Friday'. (And every Friday he wonders if those who approved his working remotely really trust him.) Work remains a destination for Bob.

He is surrounded by symbols of openness yet his behaviours don't seem to follow suit. He often walks into the office and snickers— not because he's cynical, but because he sees the irony. How is it that our modern fit-for-purpose open-plan office layout still has us emailing the person sitting a few seats away? Wasn't the purpose of the design to open communications?

Bob knows change is required. And Ms Molloy's class has made him realise that change starts with him. Change is hard because it is hard work. Change is iterative: just when you think you have changed enough, you need to change again.

But who, really, is Bob? Bob is the synthesis of many. Bob is not a bad person. Bob is busy, bombarded and in a rat race in which many days feel like a pointless pursuit. Sometimes he knows why he is doing things, sometimes he doesn't, and some days he is just going through the motions. This phenomenon is happening for Bob both at home and at work. Sometimes he is bringing his wholehearted self to work and sometimes he is just showing up as the prototype: Bob the Banker. A loose wire runs the short distance from his head to his heart—sometimes it has contact, sometimes it has short-circuited, sometimes it's sparking, and sometimes it's completely disconnected. Bob's insights lead him to understand the importance of knowing his purpose, not just as a one-off, but also as a way of living.

Some of us have amazing personal purpose but our work seems without purpose, and so our values at work and home don't align. Likewise, some of us have fantastic work purpose yet our personal purpose seems adrift, leading us to a possible double-life that is misdirected. Bob's insights regarding the purpose in his personal and work life, and the importance of their intersection, will take him out of his comfort zone. However, making that connection between his head and heart and creating alignment will be the magic ingredient for Bob in whatever role he takes on at home or at work. As a leader, a father, a husband, a community member, once Bob's made the connection people are going to be drawn to his humanity and purpose, whether they consciously realise this or not.

So on this note, we wish Bob well as he starts manifesting purpose in every aspect of his life.

Business dialogue in the class(/board)room

Teachers and parents know all too well that when a child asks *why* they are rarely seeking a black-and-white answer. They want a conversation, and if you don't give it to them they are just going to ask—wait for it—*why*. It is a word every child uses incessantly and in circles. The best response to a child's *why* has meaning and colour and presents opportunities for conversation. It is a collaboration rather than an answer or statement. It is an approach that should be applied to every business problem.

Exhausting as this may sound, Bo's classroom is not dissimilar to our meeting 'rooms' in business. Meetings and discussions that are rich with questions, and where everyone has a voice, provide rich and meaningful dialogue. Rhetorical questions, filtered listening and predetermined outcomes will close the gates to your human capital's capacity. If the heads in your boardroom are all tilting to the left, you don't have the right brain capacity to create the future. You don't have the capacity to create original ideas, ideas that bring value, or the capacity to solve what are seemingly intractable problems.

Making room for every student (and every business possibility) is critical in today's changing, challenging world.

Ms Molloy is designing for a different age—she is working for the future at a time when there is an unprecedented level of external stimulus. How is it possible for our teachers, let alone our organisations, to get and keep anyone's attention and focus? How do we keep our cultural identity intact and connect with our globalised world? How do we adapt in a rapidly changing world?

This is why it is critical that we create the environments to not just answer the question *why* but also, equally important, to enable answers to the question *how*. How we lead, how we operate and how we use technology all play significant roles in achieving our outcomes.

* * *

At such a time as this, ten years in the future is nearly impossible to predict or model. So we cannot accurately predict what our friends in Ms Molloy's class will be doing, though we have tried. But hopefully we can safely predict their ability to have clarity of purpose, connected heads and hearts, and actions that are a reflection of their intentions. Perhaps they will be the leaders of their lives.

PART III
PLOT

With earlier pages now turned and the lessons of Ms Molloy's classroom behind us, we transition to the next part of this book.

Characters and plot are the foundation of any good story. Plot is the movement in the story — it moves you through time, through the drama, through to 'the end'. Organisations need to tell their stories. Leaders: whether you're a local business owner or a CEO or a commander-in-chief, we want to hear your compelling story. People seek this. People want it to make sense. People want to connect with it. People want the narrative to reach their dreams, fears, hopes and aspirations. People want work to have meaning; otherwise aren't they just colouring inside the lines and clocking time waiting for the bell to ring? People don't want patchwork; they want life to be a tapestry. Everyone, especially Generation Y and Z, seeks more meaning, more development, more leadership and more feedback. Status and money are not enough — they want to be connected, and of course they want it now.

So if it is as simple as knowing your purpose and getting on with your business, why isn't every organisation successful?

This book addresses this question and presents a simple framework to plot the progress of your purpose and leadership in relation to the practical task of getting things done.

The PLOT Framework — **P**urpose, **L**eadership, **O**perations and **T**echnology — can be used to facilitate discussion, raise questions, challenge, gauge and monitor attainment of an on-purpose organisation. It is not your typical balanced scorecard measure; it is meant to measure the pulse of a purpose-led organisation.

This part of the book devotes a chapter to each of the four elements of the PLOT Framework and wraps it all up with an Action chapter that guides you through each quadrant of the framework. The framework acts as a gauge for your actions in relation to your intentions.

In the Action chapter you'll also find details of a couple of presentation templates to synthesise your own PLOT for your organisation, as well as a mobile application to gauge and track your progress.

CHAPTER 2

PURPOSE

I n the words of Mark Twain, 'The two most important days in your life are the day you are born and the day you find out why'.

The idea of purpose being at the heart of your life and organisation is not new. But experience and observation over 25 years shows me that where there is clear and meaningful purpose — backed with a cause — success follows.

Simply stated, having a compelling purpose defines your cause; why you exist. Purpose should have an effect on everything you do. It should be omnipresent.

It is tempting to consider purpose and meaning as pillars that are relevant only to the do-gooders of our world, the people who traditionally don't prioritise profit. These wonderful do-gooders, largely speaking, are the people who work for organisations defined by a cause. Nothing makes purpose clearer than a good dose of social injustice. So the people working to end injustice? Well, of course they have purpose and meaning.

It is easy to see how purpose is important for these organisations. Meaning oozes out of their every pore, so you would have to work hard *not* to connect with their purpose and meaning. Easy. But why, you might ask, is it so important for business, government, entrepreneurs and (dare I say) regulators to have a compelling purpose? Can purpose be made meaningful to the majority?

There is always meaning when you are doing the right thing by your constituents, whether you are working to deliver widgets, washing machines or water filtration. Meaning should be easy to identify when a moral framework is in place and a compelling purpose is present. No organisation is exempt from this paradigm.

It is tempting to think you don't need anything other than your stated purpose, but you do. Without a robust plan to operate from, you are merely stating an intention; there's no scaffolding to hold it up. Intentions without correlating actions make for lovely conversations but will not produce a measurable result. We need to move from purposeful intentions to purposeful action.

The core

Where to start? Always start at the top! (Says my inner Dr Seuss.)

A leader without a purpose is a lost leader. As Yogi Berra once said, 'If you don't know where you're going, you'll end up some place else'.

We cannot afford to have leaders whose purpose is not clear, or leaders who have a wobbly ethical and moral framework.

To create a purpose-led organisation, leaders at every level need to believe in its compelling purpose. That's how they develop a sense of ownership, frame an effective vision, build capacity and, most importantly, foster and enable a supportive environment.

What gets really exciting is when we understand that a shared purpose creates consequences that go beyond the individual—

and, in a world of growing self-interest and individualism, we need all the help we can get. It is hard to make everyone feel like they belong; it is hard to make everyone feel connected. But when you have a purpose that's demonstrated through honest humanity and that stands on a strong ethical foundation, you will create trust.

People value trust over information. As such, a community will naturally build around your leaders, with your shared purpose at its centre.

Our purpose, be it personal or organisational, must answer key questions—the *whys*. We must ask the tough *why* questions to distil a purpose down to its purest and noblest goal.

Your purpose should:

- define your reason to exist

- pervade vision and strategy

- provide intrinsic measures of success.

Your reason to exist

A well-written purpose should define your cause, as well as the character of people you need to work with as a purposeful collective to achieve it.

Note the choice of words: 'work with'. In our connected world, the definition of 'internal' is blurring fast, so include everyone who contributes to your customer's experience—starting with your supply chain. Working in community with your supply chain (rather than just exchanging invoices) will elevate your level of engagement and enable you to move from the transactional to the relational. And if the forces within your supply chain do not relate to your purpose, what *do* they relate to—just a price point?

Consider the collective impact of working with people of consistent character. It's the greatest input to your overall culture (after all, people are your cultural fuel). What do I mean by 'consistent character'? I am referring to your values and principles in action. Not a room full of people like you (PLU)—the dreaded PLU culture is one of the last things I would encourage!

Consistent character does *not* exclude diversity—it should actually enhance it. No decent organisation thinks that hiring 'people like us' will help them beat their competitors. At every level of your organisation, a diversity of thought, gender, ethnicity and circumstance will give depth and richness to your purpose—and, as an added bonus, your team will most likely reflect the diversity of your customer base.

The reason I include circumstance as a specific area of diversity is that I often wonder about the bias against the single parent, the not-partnered, or those without children. If you're in one of these categories, I think you know what I mean. Inclusiveness is so much more than a buzzword, and we should be mindful of this in a very real and practical way: we all benefit when true diversity is brought into action.

To build our organisations' character and culture, to embed the values and principles underpinning our purpose, we need to move from the 'to have' to the more simple and heartfelt 'to be'.

We need to be the sum of who we are, *not what we* have.

When we move from having to being, we create a culture that expresses creativity, engenders relationships and shares openly. Intangible shared values become tangible through culture.

See through vision, direct through strategy

Vision is your future state.

It should give everyone the ability to imagine the purpose fulfilled. Great leaders translate purpose into a powerfully framed vision.

In the past, setting vision has often been linked with the 'visionary': the leader with charisma, or the alpha-CEO. But it is important that vision stands on its own two feet—otherwise it can quite easily walk out the door with the leader.

In *Built to Last*, their book about visionary companies, Jim Collins and Jerry I. Porras refer to 'Big, Hairy, Audacious Goals' (or BHAGs). BHAGs can be used to make your purpose (and mission, if one is stated) come to life.

Vision, or BHAG (call it what works best for you) should paint the glorious picture of your purpose being realised. You may at some stage have to alter the picture, but purpose is your constant, your anchor.

So. How do you bring any great story to an audience? The director. The director pulls it all together, never losing sight of what that amazing story is going to look like on the big screen. Strategy directs by bringing the purpose to life—it is your cunning plan.

Your cunning plan needs to be designed to achieve your purpose. While it may seem like an obvious point to make, it is incredible how this purpose anchor can slip when details start to kick in. Your purpose must always be at the heart of your strategic thinking—its concepts, policies, goals, processes, decisions, and so on.

It is important that vision stands on its own two feet; otherwise it can quite easily walk out the door with the leader.

Your strategy will serve your customers and stakeholders, define your competitive points of difference and work to achieve your measures of success (tangible and intangible). And when a strategy changes, which it will over time, it is important to review your organisational design and structure. If your culture can shock-absorb these types of changes you know you are anchored in purpose.

Visions and strategies may change, be calibrated or pivot, but purpose must be your constant. So spend the time to get it right and align everything and everyone to it.

Intrinsic measures of success

Amazing things happen when you create meaning for people, or when people find meaning in what they do day-to-day. Your organisation's combined purpose, vision and strategy should articulate and espouse meaning, values and principles. If it doesn't, don't be surprised if people seek it elsewhere.

Every intrinsic measure of success serves to lift our spirits. The pay slip is no longer the payoff. People need to feel heard and validated. Accountability and responsibility have replaced reporting lines. Big companies are full of dotted reporting lines, but everyone in a start-up thinks 'hierarchy' is a mediaeval Latin word. The barriers and boundaries of 'self' have become permeable, creating the possibility for incredible collaboration and innovation.

You are creating your community—so bring everyone in the food chain along with you! The human potential is the most underutilised resource in most organisations. Tap into it by harnessing everyone's dreams, creativity, aspirations and emotions. It may feel scary but it will release a powerful competitive difference that is impossible to replicate on a 3D printer.

The best thing about creating meaning is it creates happiness. Quite simply, happiness feeds the human soul, which in turn boosts organisations' success.

THE DIFFERENCE BETWEEN PURPOSE AND MISSION

Many organisations have mission statements. GameChangers 500 posts each of its members' mission statements online. (It's a great reference site for creating or calibrating your purpose, by the way.) These are amazing organisations with amazing missions.

But before we continue, what is the difference between purpose and mission? The definitions are very close, so in theory you can have either, or have both. So why should you have a stated purpose? Why not just state your mission?

People associate the word 'mission' (which comes from the Latin *mittere*, meaning 'to send') with being 'on a mission', whether that be in service of their convictions, for war or for religion.

'Purpose' is a word people say in their day-to-day lives. You will be hard-pressed to hear people in the corridor or café speaking about their mission, but you *will* hear the word 'purpose', in all its glorious idioms and forms.

The word 'mission', while derived from a verb, is a noun. The word 'purpose' is both a noun and a verb.

At the risk of sounding pedantic, I believe verbs provoke action so much more acutely than nouns. It may be somewhat quirky, but 'purpose' denotes action for me. Purpose provides a grounded context in which people can live and work.

Some people love their mission statements, and if this is you, by all means have one. But use it solely to add depth, colour and richness to your purpose. And don't expect people to remember it as well as they will remember your simple and powerful purpose with meaning.

(continued)

THE DIFFERENCE BETWEEN
PURPOSE AND MISSION *(cont'd)*

To be honest, though, the better outcome is to do away with half of your published statements and simply let the purpose shine on its own — clearly and memorably as it deserves to, for the sake of everyone involved.

If you have to have both a mission and a purpose:

- ensure your mission outlines your *intentions*

- project a clear purpose to produce *actions*

- combine both and you will thrive with *meaning*.

Real-life stories

In my experience, your intention to serve your customer must be stated in your purpose if you really want your customer at the heart of everything you do.

You would assume that all businesses in the service industry have the customer at the heart of their purpose. Some do, some don't. You will know those who don't, as it typically hurts to do business with them. You don't receive exceptional service, and you're lucky to get good service. All is dependent on the specific individual who serves you — it has nothing to do with the organisation as a whole.

There is a raft of research on everything we just went through but, as you might have gathered by now, I'm a big believer in the stories behind the theory. Here are some real-life experiences that demonstrate the impact of purpose (or lack thereof).

—————————————— CASE STUDY ——————————————

Company 1 — customers at the heart
Our purpose is to consistently and reliably deliver excellent service to our customers

While this is not rocket science — and the statement may not make you feel like it would transform a business in today's environment — it was progressive for the 1990s when it appeared in the IT industry. By focusing not on the business mechanics, per se, but on the people affected by the business, it immediately became more meaningful.

What's more, this purpose was defined during a time when suppliers sold service agreements with service-level commitments ... but thought it was perfectly okay to have essential spare parts centrally located *away* from their clients. How can you get a replacement installed in four hours if the part is eight hours away?

Did this simple statement have an impact? Absolutely. Why? Because the statement of purpose was used throughout all levels of the organisation to query its service delivery. It came at a time when standards for the IT industry were being set.

If you have committed to restore a customer's IT infrastructure within two hours of a detected or reported outage, for example, then you need to invest in the infrastructure to achieve this — consistently and reliably.

Not by chance, not by luck, but with calculated investments that range from supplier agreements to spare parts and engineering resourcing and so on. This is where operations need to support your purpose, to take it out of the realm of high ideals and lip service and into the nuts and bolts of business workflows.

(continued)

Company 1 — customers at the heart *(cont'd)*

This may seem obvious. But many people believe that service levels are a statistical calculation rather than a defined process. If it had paid attention only to the number—not the process and what it means for the customer—this company would have fallen short every time. It would have undermined its own long-term revenue, because unhappy customers would have voted with their feet.

A simple statement of purpose enables you to challenge anyone who is calculating a price or decision based on a service level. The service providers in IT thinned out pretty quickly after the dotcom crash; all of a sudden, delivery became a strategic imperative. It is no coincidence that user experience and customer experience is all-important in this day and age.

The way this company worded its purpose is important. Imagine if the word 'reliably' or 'consistently' hadn't been included. Without 'reliably' in the purpose statement, you leave room for individual interpretation of what excellent service means. Is 'excellent' okay most of the time, or 99.999% of the time?

These five nines—the 99.999%—are what customers expect when they purchase a 99.999% service level commitment in their service contract. Service providers need to build the capacity to meet the promise. 'Reliably' and 'consistently' are critical words here.

--- CASE STUDY ---

Company 2 — misguided purpose
Our purpose is to get the stock price to $100

In this example, a new executive team was hired for the merger of two IT organisations. The new CEO arrived with charisma, energy and a successful track record—enough to make him a 'rock star' rather than a 'roll your sleeves up' kind of guy.

The new leadership team was built without either founder from the merging organisations on board; however, key people were promoted and a few of the new CEO's close colleagues and friends were brought in.

The purpose statement was clear: to get the stock price to $100. It was about $30 when the merger was announced.

The troops rallied. The purpose seemingly had meaning to many, as it tapped into their stock options — something that everyone working for a 1990s start-up had, or aspired to have. Everyone loved the new leadership team and the energy that poured out of them.

The purpose was without a customer and without a cause. It was a misguided purpose. It was aimed squarely at shareholders and those employees who had shares. It was also aimed at the executive leadership team, as they had shares as a key component of their compensation package.

With the beauty of hindsight it's easy to see how this was going to play out. The company's stock did indeed hit $100 and the leadership team sold out. Key executives sat at their desks counting their stock options and the company started to fall into rapid decline.

The competitor, still run by its founder, stomped on the opportunity. The company was sold and the purchasing organisation's fate was bankruptcy. It's not surprising, looking back now, but perhaps if the attention had been on-purpose, with more inclusivity and meaning, it would have ended differently.

The moral of the story is that if your purpose is simply to meet a financial objective you may well fail. Your budget, stock price and profit need to be successful, but they are the result of your cause. They are not your reason for being.

Start with the cause

Existing organisations need to thread everything together.

Start by calibrating or creating the cause that drives your purpose. All organisations can have a cause—you don't have to be a not-for-profit or social enterprise—and all organisations should. It is hard to inspire your people to achieve great things if their personal goals don't connect with the organisational goals. When your customer is part of your purpose you can always find a cause, a cause that everyone should connect with.

This is because creating a purpose that puts your customer front and centre will very likely bond personal values and work values for many employees. And if putting the customer up front and centre doesn't reflect the values of your employees, then perhaps they should be working for another organisation with another purpose.

That may sound strong but the point is valid. Whether the driving cause of your purpose is a customer, a charity or a way of viewing the world, an employee who doesn't resonate with this is better placed in another role outside the organisation. Your purpose will attract the right people to your company: people who are excited to work with your organisation and who, quite literally, support the cause.

As outlined earlier, if you have a stated mission that you like, then keep it, but create an overarching purpose statement and link these two together. If you just stick with a mission you risk losing that guiding principle—and then this proposed framework becomes MLOT or PMLOT. Personally, I like PLOT a *lot* better.

Next, review everything else you have published—vision statements, values, external marketing activities, and cascade their meaning from your new purpose. It will be a beautiful puzzle that fits together with purpose at the heart of everything, and your customers, culture and collateral will thank you for it.

Taking the time to review or create your purpose is to plot a journey for success, no matter what your organisation does. Taking time to look at your personal purpose will reset your course along a road worth travelling. This in itself is a massive topic with an enormous body of work devoted to it, from *Being and Nothingness* by Jean-Paul Sartre to *Man's Search for Meaning* by Viktor E. Frankl. It is by no means simple.

The point here is that for any organisation to achieve greatness, we need people who know their purpose and people who are leading with humanity. The better you encourage this within your company, the greater your chance of success.

Find the meaning

It is not uncommon to come across people who just don't believe you can instil meaning into their purpose.

I have met many people who believe this, from entrepreneurs and public servants to corporate executives. And the story goes something like this: 'We just aren't like Company XYZ who does really important work for society'.

I challenge anyone. If your desire is to create meaning for your stakeholders, you will find meaning.

And what is meaning in the context of an organisation?

When your spotlight is on the customer you can start to anticipate their needs. You will always meet their needs, wants and expectations, and then slowly start to exceed them. Your cause does not *have* to be linked with social reform or community giving, but it does have to be centred on your customer in some way.

Many companies link their purpose with other needs in the world. While a social purpose is often the desired end state, it will find its way into the fabric of your organisation as part of an ethical, humane, customer-oriented purpose. Without the customers and the revenue, the social purpose might not be met.

Listen to the calling of your employees

With Venn diagrams all over the internet intersecting everyone's personal vocations and passions, how can our employees seek their own calling within an organisation's purpose?

To cite some words of wisdom from Martin Luther King, Jr: 'No work is insignificant. All labor that uplifts humanity has dignity and importance and should be undertaken with painstaking excellence'.

Your organisation may not be where the person's longer-term vocation lies, but that doesn't mean their work cannot be meaningful in the meantime. When you set a purpose to *create* purpose and meaning, you will no doubt impart some meaning to everyone along the way, whether they work for you for a summer holiday, or for a lifetime.

For some context here, let's dive into an example that reflects an experience familiar to many of us.

You are working in the hospitality industry, in a local café, for the café owner. You know this work is not your passion, nor is it your vocation. As a matter of fact, you are struggling to find any purpose other than to fund a short-term goal.

There are two ways the café owner could approach this scenario:

Café 1. The owner is disgruntled and tired. All they want to do is to maximise profits so they can sell the business in three years. There is no meaning in this purpose, no humanity, no collaboration between staff and customers and, arguably, less of a sense of ethics.

Café 2. The business owner believes that the desires and experiences of the customer are all that matter. They source the best-tasting (and financially viable) coffee beans available and ensure each coffee is made with precise care. They get great joy out of knowing that the simple act of making someone a coffee can genuinely brighten their day. They lead their café from the front, embracing and celebrating their customers by making it a happy, relaxing place. They are looking forward to selling the business in three years.

Two purposes, same desired end state. Which café would you rather work for? As a customer, from which café would you rather buy your guilty pleasure of coffee and cake (something you look forward to all week)?

Or, to switch this around, let's say you are the café owner. Everyone who works for you is paid the minimum wage and everyone has vocations outside of hospitality — you are simply paying their bills for a while. How do you get your team of employees to celebrate work every day and make customers into raving fans?

Do you run the café with people lining up to get in the door, or are you just a convenient stop-off location for disengaged customers? Does making and serving coffee become artisan work that enriches the experience of those who work for you and those you serve? Or are your employees so unhappy they leave each day steeped in drudgery, unable to hide the sour energy from your customers, no matter how hard they try?

No doubt you have been to both cafés in your lifetime, several times over. And regardless of whether you drink coffee or not, the business scenario could apply to most consumer goods and services.

The book *Fish!: A Remarkable Way to Boost Morale and Improve Results* by Stephen Lundin, Harry Paul and John Christensen was a bestseller. Why? Because everyone — employees, customers and business owners — would prefer to be in Café 2. The warm atmosphere in Café 2 comes from a collective culture and unified purpose exuded by all the employees, from the full-time barista to the part-time waiter.

* * *

In our converging global world of instant sharing, borderless collaboration, mobilised collectives and virtual communities, you have to trust that organisations that are working for the benefit of their customers will reign over those who are myopic to a single stakeholder—be it the shareholder, the owner or the party. The right purpose will lead you to the right outcome.

The *why* of your purpose has been well chronicled. Our job is to flesh out the *how*, so that it has meaning in your day-to-day life.

Snapshot: Quick guide (if that's even possible) to being on-purpose

1 Before doing anything, get online and measure your own personal values (perhaps try www.valuescentre.com). This will help you understand how you connect with your organisation's purpose—or not!

2 Connect home and the office. Get to know your personal purpose and how it relates to your work.

3 If you are a leader in an organisation, define or refine your purpose. If you are working in an organisation, make sure you know its purpose.

4 If needed, a mission statement should be used to deepen and enrich your cause.

5 Create a vision so you are able to realistically imagine the future state and outcomes of your cause. It sets the direction.

6 Design a strategy to act as a detailed plan to give life to your purpose, mission and vision.

7 Infuse everything you do with humanity, meaning and ethics, so that everyone is inspired, connected and committed.

8 Connect. Communication is an essential ingredient to success. Keep it simple, make it accessible and share. Think community. Check out chapter 6 (Action) for more information.

CHAPTER 3
LEADERSHIP

E veryone has a reaction to the word 'leadership', and rightly so. There is nothing new or surprising about this. Given that it is so well researched, and there's so much great reading freely available to us all, why does it go so wrong and why is it so hard to get right? Why the dearth?

Let's start by acknowledging that time is a key commitment; it is vital to make the time to be better leaders — time for ourselves and for those around us. Stress, pressure, world events, life: they all impact what we do. And then we get hit with everything that comes with being human — from our fortitudes to our flaws.

I am neither a philosopher nor a psychiatrist, nor do I pretend to be, so I reach out to the many experts.

C. G. Jung gave us the concepts of archetypes, the collective unconscious, extraversion and introversion. These are key concepts in a world where human capital — knowledge and thinking — are your competitive advantage. Quoting Jung helps frame leadership as something that is collective rather than individual: 'The meeting of two personalities is like the contact of two chemical substances: if there is any reaction, both are transformed'. Transformational leadership is the new minimum standard.

Power made by many

Traditional models of leadership are changing. The changes may not have taken hold in every corporation, but they certainly have in fast-growing start-ups. In these nimble worlds, hierarchy is architecture, not a reporting line.

In 'Understanding "New Power"', an article published by *Harvard Business Review*, Jeremy Heimans and Henry Timms provide an interesting perspective on these shifts, powered by ones and zeroes.

> *Old power* works like a currency. It is held by few. Once gained, it is jealously guarded, and the powerful have a substantial store of it to spend. It is closed, inaccessible, and leader-driven. It downloads, and it captures.

> *New power* operates differently, like a current. It is made by many. It is open, participatory, and peer-driven. It uploads, and it distributes. Like water or electricity, it's most forceful when it surges. The goal with new power is not to hoard it but to channel it.

Weaving old and new power together through a common thread of purpose emboldens everyone, averting a collision course of any potentially misguided, individual intentions.

Could it be that modern neuroscience powered by technology is helping everyone rise above circumstance? As Jung put it, 'I am not what happened to me, I am what I choose to become'.

As discussed in Otto Scharmer's book *Theory U*, the Indo-European root of the verb 'to lead' is 'leith'—to step across a threshold and let go of whatever might limit us stepping forward. If we can let go, step forward and choose to do this, we can all be the leaders of our own lives.

With this mindset of personal leadership, organisation-wide leadership becomes possible when unified by purpose and values. Perhaps if everyone saw themselves as leaders there would be shifts in the world to solve the intractable?

Awaken to the leader inside you, and help everyone else awaken to theirs. Leaders come from anywhere and everywhere — from the streets of New York City to the villages of rural India. You will most certainly have followers and followership (people taking your lead), you just might not be aware of it.

We are the leaders of our lives.

So, what does a world look like when everyone sees themselves as the leaders of their lives?

When you awaken from within and become responsible and accountable as your own life's leader, you are the main character in your story: you are writing the plot. If everyone is encouraged to have this mindset in an organisation led by a unifying, meaningful purpose, the right ingredients are there for everyone to flourish together.

So what goes wrong? Let's start at the top. The extreme example looks like an old-power leadership model with misguided leaders at the helm, eroding and potentially crushing the human spirit. Somewhere in the middle lies the compromised, materialising as mediocrity, hubris and cynicism. These are the cracks that eventually create the gaps that land us in all sorts of troubled water.

If we are trying to move to the new power 'made by many' model we need leaders who are epiphytes rather than parasites — where your means is not their end. In nature there are parasites capable of changing the social behaviour of their hosts at both an individual and group interaction level! When people are connecting with the purpose, they will not feel, nor be, a means to an end. The idea of 'a leader', one hero that saves the day, will not work for the knowledge worker. Our knowledge workers seek purpose, mastery and autonomy.

Co-creating leadership

Our leaders need to define purpose, frame vision, develop strategy and engender the character—the values and principles—required to execute. They need to live the values and principles; move away from *reaction* and towards *co-creation*. At the same time they need to manage—sometimes ruthlessly—the hard truths underlying today's problems before any purpose can be realised.

Great leaders operate at a visceral level. They are in the trenches, they are experiencing their customers' touch points, they are meeting their stakeholders, and they are literally learning at the feet of those who struggle the most.

Before you make the policies, experience the practices within them. That working parent policy? Try getting the bus to childcare for an 8.30 am drop-off before a 9 am meeting, and see whether there needs to be more humanity throughout the organisation, to reflect your purpose. Or it may be about ensuring that diversity is more than a buzzword, that it is experienced rather than just talked about. Whatever it is, experience the policies you are looking to implement on a real-life, meaningful level, so that you can walk a day in the shoes of those you are wanting to engage.

Here are some simple leadership steps to start with:

- Define your purpose and get on-purpose. Purpose precedes everything—from accountability to measures. Form follows function.

- Know who you need to *be* to lead on-purpose.

- Find leaders who espouse the values and principles of your purpose—people who know themselves, their purpose and their values.

- Engender the collective.

- Embed and infuse purpose in your PLOT; that is, in everything you do—strategically, operationally and technically. Inspect what you expect.

- Celebrate the past, present and future: celebrate, measure, reflect, calibrate, integrate and, just as importantly, celebrate again! (Never underestimate the importance of small acts of recognition. There's no need to wait for the awards night: see figure 3.1.)

Figure 3.1: celebration circle

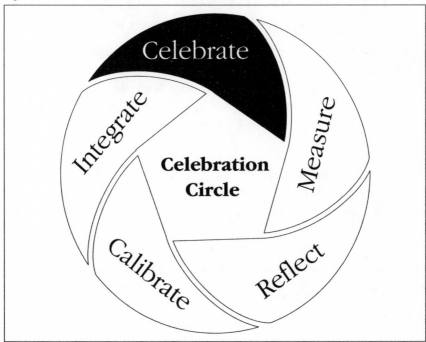

The real challenge is that the nature and level of commitment required in leadership is *relentless*.

But what if everyone was working at a collective level? What if we got the right people in the right places and everyone around them worked collectively, on-purpose, for success?

Complications

If leadership were easy the world would be in better shape. But it's not easy. Things get complicated.

Let's unpack a few examples you might encounter along the way.

Purpose is circumvented by capital-market disciplines

When short-term financial performance and current shareholder value dominate the minds of our leaders the risk is that unstated (and perhaps even unconscious) bias becomes the focus and purpose is subtly sidelined in the process. Leaders need to be the stewards of multiple interests—one very visible, visceral number cannot be all we serve.

The most powerful purpose gets undermined with detrimental and pernicious effects. Creativity, innovation, strategy, policies, principles and, most importantly, morality and meaning, are blocked by shareholder-driven thinking, putting the short-term 'wins' in front of longer term growth. It starts ever so slowly, without impacting the short-term results, so those at the top of the organisation—the very source of the problem—may not even notice.

To counter the potential for going off-purpose, many organisations conduct surveys to measure the multitude of soft indicators and issues that affect performance. Sometimes, however, particularly when mediocrity has set in, the results are benign, if rarely that insightful, despite the disconnect going on. It is not until you are off the cliff that the survey screams out the truth.

It is important, of course, to measure and reward your organisation's achievement by and through its purpose. Dictionary.com defines performance as 'the manner in which or the efficiency with which something reacts or fulfils its intended purpose'. *Everything* stems from your purpose, including the way you define performance and the way your leaders need to *be*.

Performance is not just your share price. Performance is not just your profit. And most importantly a pay-for-performance philosophy, where pay is commensurate with contribution, needs to be consistent throughout your organisation.

The majority now agree that short-term thinking and a single measure are short-sighted as we enter the long-cited third macro-level transformation in human history.

Icebergs (there's a lot under that tip)

Before beginning, we nod respectfully to the vast literature on the topic of the human mind, from the world's great philosophers and scientists to today's behavioural and organisational sciences and expansive neuroscience fields.

Social and psychological biases impact every aspect of life. They create judgements. They steer decisions. Fact.

The iceberg model, traced to Sigmund Freud's Iceberg Model of Consciousness, is widely used to help understand why people do what they do.

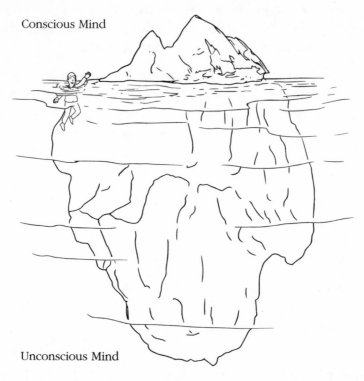

Conscious Mind

Unconscious Mind

Freud's iceberg metaphor illustrates the 10 per cent of our psyche that's visible—the tip of our iceberg—alongside the 90 per cent of our mind that is subconscious, or unconscious. Our true mental nature lies mostly underwater, so to speak. I like to call this our 'underberg'.

Understanding what is beneath our own waterline enables the leader within to push through. But beware: there always seem to be a lot of fears under that tip. To counter this, I always revert to the words of Franklin D. Roosevelt: '...the only thing we have to fear is fear itself', and to Marianne Williamson's magnificent poem *Our Deepest Fear.*

THE OPEN-DOOR ICEBERG

As leaders, we should all try to encourage what I call the open-door iceberg. One of the best parts of working with an open-door iceberg — meaning that what is under your iceberg is discussed openly and shared as part of your personal development — is its sheer transparency and honesty.

Everyone has stuff under water. Once it's disclosed, we grow together.

I worked with a colleague for over seven years. One of the biases sitting under her iceberg manifested in her inability to receive any constructive criticism; if a mistake was made, blame sometimes surfaced.

We agreed that understanding and addressing this would be a personal development goal. We focused on getting to the root cause in a trusted and safe environment. During her childhood she had climbed into the car with her brother, pretending to drive. She took the handbrake off. The car rolled back and crashed. Luckily no-one was hurt, but you can bet she was blamed. Alas, the trigger was set.

We referred to this fear-driven trigger as 'a handbrake moment'. It became our cut-through for crucial conversations and for receiving critical feedback.

It is extremely difficult to change behaviours without understanding or addressing the underlying mindset or the unmet needs behind them.

Continuing with the open-door iceberg metaphor, as we travel deep into the sea under our own iceberg it can get very dark: immorality, selfishness, violence, shameful experiences, socially unacceptable behaviours—the list goes on.

---

*Everybody, no matter who they are or what they do, has an underberg.
Some just run deeper and darker than others.*

Cognitive bias brings another layer of complexity. This will not be explored in this book, and I don't pretend to be an expert. But what is essential is that leaders get to know people better, have relationships with them and have an understanding of their needs and fears. The paradox is that with a need there is often an associated fear—the classic being the need for achievement accompanied on its dark side by a fear of failure.

MY UNDERBERG MOMENT

My underberg realisation came while I was in Rajasthan, India, leading a leadership program for 20 executives in partnership with The Hunger Project.

The Elected Women Representatives we met are amazing women who are trained to set a vision, make commitments and then act. They are the most fearless women I have ever encountered. This is transformational leadership in action. Please visit The Hunger Project's website and find out more, as this simple statement doesn't do justice to its work.

Witnessing the Elected Women Representatives' fearless approach to everything they aspired to, moving past injustice, poverty and every other obstacle in their way, catalysed a review of my own fears.

Understanding my fears and needs, and openly sharing them in the context of leadership development, has given me courage to step out of my comfort zone, which was previously holding me back.

Out from under the berg I go!

So pull the rug out from under your berg and boldly share. A leader sharing their whole self opens the door for everyone else to face, and shift, their own underbergs.

Positions of power and perilous pressure

Let's talk about leaders who currently hold power—whether that be political, financial, hierarchical or something else. They are often in the spotlight. This in itself can be exhausting. Every facial expression, every gesture, every action is up for interpretation (and if you're a woman...well that's another book).

The following scenarios are illustrations of the kind of small, most likely innocent, 'cracks' that create impact or get interpreted as symbols of something much bigger.

ENTREPRENEUR PEP TALK

An entrepreneur is investing in your company and has been given the floor to present the reasons why they are putting their money into your business.

It's a big moment. Your entire team is present and eagerly awaiting the heartfelt speech that will possibly affect their future.

Instead of a speech rich in purpose and meaning for the collective, the entrepreneur opens with a statement of personal wealth creation and follows on with an overview of the workload for the next six months.

You can imagine the reaction. How to disenfranchise the entire room in 30 seconds.

EXECUTIVE PEP TALK

The executive walks into the crowded room to announce how important the leadership workshop is — the one they have just entered. They pop in, give their ten-minute presentation and then leave, stating that they can't stay. They offer no details as to why they can't stay, or perhaps it's just that the reason they give doesn't seem as important as your personal development.

The alternative scenario, the one that actually happened, is that the leader believes in the leadership program they have developed. The leader carves ample time out of their diary to make sure they are participating at all levels. Leadership is not something that gets outsourced to a third party or to the internal teams; it is something they hold themselves accountable to. Everything they say and do is a symbol of their commitment.

The leader knows that people are the greatest resource, and that being hands-on makes all the difference. They are immersed in the design and outcomes of the leadership programs. Oh, and of course they stay for the entire workshop.

Intention and attention are both needed in leadership if we are to stop the gap. I guess we truly have to mind the gap.

What else gets in the way? Answers lie in the spectrum of our humanity, from the hidden to the forgotten. The extreme is that we forget to bring our humanity to work. Or perhaps we bring it some days and other days, well, other things seem to dominate.

Or we hide. We hide our humanity in the name of being the all-powerful, strong leader. We are all imperfect beings, so bring your imperfections to work as well. Be emotionally honest. Read Brené Brown's books. Share your hopes, dreams, fears, anxieties, and grief. Be a human, role independent.

A word on self-interest: for leaders in power, self-interest needs to be an unnatural state.

The pursuit of self-interest is not in the job description. We must be pursuing the betterment of the collective. In a research report from McKinsey & Company titled 'How leaders kill meaning at work', Teresa Amabile and Steven Kramer note that 'senior executives routinely undermine creativity, productivity, and commitment by damaging the inner work lives of their employees in four avoidable ways':

1 mediocrity signals — inadvertently signalling the opposite of your purpose through your words and actions

2 strategic 'attention deficit disorder' — starting and stopping too frequently, creating an appearance that the leader doesn't have their act together

3 corporate 'keystone cops' (fictional police running in circles) — inadequate coordination and support to achieve a high quality outcome

4 misbegotten Big, Hairy, Audacious Goals — creating BHAGs that are grandiose, unattainable or so vague as to seem empty.

'Inner work life' is defined as the constant flow of emotions, motivations and perceptions that constitute a person's reactions to the events of the work day. Impacting 'inner work life' impacts people's ability to be and stay on-purpose. It can be avoided, but it requires constant attention to detail to do so; undermining is corrosive by nature.

The small things we do matter, particularly when it comes to meaning at work.

Meaning is catching

Being open to having people present ideas on how you can improve meaning at work is just as important as sourcing ideas on how to improve your business processes, your client experience or your next innovation. They are all equally important.

Meaning at work has an amazing knock-on effect. It spreads like a virus and even the most pessimistic people catch it! Collective purpose and meaning create cohesion, drop barriers, expand the pursuit beyond the self, and feed the soul of your colleagues. Meaning lasts beyond work hours; it keeps us connected and collaborating even when we are no longer working together.

Do people really care? Apparently, they do. There is significant research on this subject, but I quite like the *Harvard Business Review* summary 'Connect, Then Lead' by Amy J. C. Cuddy, Matthew Kohut and John Neffinger:

> Is it better to be loved or feared? Niccolò Machiavelli pondered that timeless conundrum 500 years ago and hedged his bets. 'It may be answered that one should wish to be both,' he acknowledged, 'but because it is difficult to unite them in one person, it is much safer to be feared than loved.'
>
> Now behavioural science is weighing in with research showing that Machiavelli had it partly right: When we judge others — especially our leaders — we look first at two characteristics: how lovable they are (their warmth, communion, or trustworthiness) and how fearsome they are (their strength, agency, or competence)…
>
> Why are these traits so important? Because they answer two critical questions: 'What are this person's intentions toward me?' and 'Is he or she capable of acting on those intentions?'

The cut-through from the article is that warmth trumps strength. Don't look to be feared as a leader: true strength doesn't lie in being feared.

So, what to be?

So, warmth trumps strength when we look at our leaders. It sounds easy doesn't it? But if this is so easy, why isn't every leader embodying warmth?

Warmth is hard even for the warmest of people. On a cold day when you are a bit cranky and you're behind on your numbers, where's the warmth going to come from? If you were raised to think that strength trumps warmth, what personal development program can really help with that deep-seated belief?

These are the normal human conditions that impact our workplace every day. And on top of it all there are going to be days when pure strength is needed. Combining warmth and strength is not easy.

As much as I enjoyed the Cuddy, Kohut and Neffinger article on warmth, I could not help but laugh at the 'Are You Projecting Warmth?' diagrams noted as best practice. Not wanting to poke fun, but in my experience the easiest way to project warmth is to *be* warm.

We have to *be* what we are trying to project.

Which self are you putting forward?

If personal pursuit is centred on the self this is going to be very difficult. If your primary agenda is the next promotion, or personal wealth, or personal brand, grabbing a Brené Brown book at the airport and trying to be authentic is not going to work. Authenticity will not project.

You will project what you seek. Someone who is pretending to be authentic is much worse than an inauthentic leader. It actually escalates distrust and, for those with a sense of humour—well, it's just very funny.

To be an authentic leader you have to be authentic.

So if you enter a room as your warm, humane self, why is it so hard as a leader to create meaning at work? Much as is the case for parents, your every move is watched. For senior executives, personal touch points are few and far between, so your every move matters. A simple jest if not on-purpose may be misinterpreted.

We are all human, we all have bad days, we all make mistakes—so how can you manage misinterpretations?

Opening the door

We need to let people know if we are having a bad day, and we need to declare mistakes. Chips on shoulders need to be unpacked—they cannot be everyone's burden to bear. Create an environment where people can show you your flaws, and everyone flourishes.

When you open the door to your humanity, humans walk through it.

This is the hardest part of the PLOT Framework. Anyone who is 'in power' holds the responsibility to create, lead and maintain a meaningful purpose. This responsibility is one of morality, and also business strategy. When you are chartered with being responsible to your customers, employees, shareholders, suppliers and communities, the outcome will mostly be determined by the success of your human capital.

To support this you need to unleash the potential of everyone around you and create a leadership mindset. In the words of Leo Tolstoy, 'Everyone thinks of changing the world, but no one thinks of changing himself'.

Great leaders open the door to possibility.

The power of the mind

What is your mindset? Your organisation's mindset? From the Cold War mindset to the Collective, the range is endless. Creating a mindset that espouses a positive, optimistic approach to fulfilling your purpose is essential. It's easy to talk about, hard to do—especially on those days when everything seems to be leading you down the negative-mindset rabbit hole.

Automatic negative thoughts can create the reality of our experiences as powerfully as performance enhancing thoughts.

Or, as neuroscientist Dr John Medina advises, 'Replace the CVS with the BVS'. That is, replace your current view of the situation with the better view of the situation. Do this at least 100 times a day, he advises, and your brain will physically change in response to the significant shift in your thought patterns. This simple sing-song piece of advice could be life-changing.

A word on transformation

Transformation is a word that cynics roll their eyes at, optimists look forward to—and bacteria? Well, for bacteria it's an opportunity to receive some exogenous genetic material. But even bacteria must be in a state of competence for transformation to take place!

Profound change, innovation and sustainable leadership are all requirements in today's connected world. The work of C. Otto Scharmer, covered in the next section, provides guidance on becoming transformational leaders—leaders of others, and of our own lives.

This is achieved by raising awareness, reflecting and then turning those intentions into action. These are the simple steps that help shift us up the curve so to speak. This matters because, in the words of Albert Einstein, 'The world we have made, as a result of the level of thinking we have done thus far, creates problems we cannot solve at the same level of thinking at which we created them'.

Theory U

With all this in mind, I'd like to introduce you to Otto Scharmer's Theory U (see figure 3.2, overleaf), if you are not already familiar with it.

Figure 3.2: Theory U

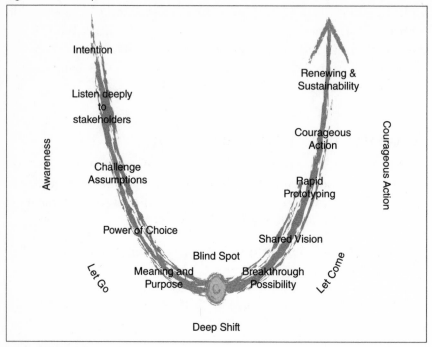

Source: © Otto Scharmer.

Do you know your blind spots?

Let's start with our blind spot, at the bottom of the U. This is the key point of insight—the point at which there is the opportunity for effective leadership to translate into social action.

Blind spots aren't necessarily bad things; they just get in the way of the perfectly balanced circuitry that is a strong head-and-heart connection.

Are any of these simple examples you?

SOUND FAMILIAR?

The shambolic. Do you forget birthdays? Are you late for meetings? Do you forget people's names? Become or hire the ultimate concierge.

The 'A' type. Ticking all the boxes is your idea of success. You try to *make* change happen. Your head may get the job done but the team might not be standing beside you, let alone behind you.

The fixer. Great at problem-solving and fixing things, but not co-creating a new future. Everyone needs to come with you — and fixing is not innovating.

The helpful 'yes' guy. Can't say no? Work on how to set boundaries and how to say no. Always say no with good reason, and remember to let your yes be yes and your no be no.

The roadrunner. 'I'm so busy' is your mantra. You are addicted to being busy. So busy you run out of time for everybody, including yourself. No-one seems to win, but your health always seems to be the biggest loser.

Be the torch-bearer

Once you tackle your blind spot(s) honestly, transparently and with courage, work on being a torch-bearer for change.

Regardless of where you are on the Theory U curve, no matter your blind spots, your meaningful purpose is your cornerstone. It will carry you onwards and upwards, so that you can hold the flame—and a single flame lights many. When the work you do becomes a pathway and instrument for personal meaning and achievement, then everyone is moving up the curve together.

This role is not easy and it carries a heavy weight. Tirelessly building your organisation's character is exhausting. In the words of Winston Churchill, 'Success is never final'.

It all starts with courage

There is a raft of leadership foundations one must have in life, but start with courage.

It takes enormous courage to put the cause, the purpose, over your career. It takes just as much courage to move from self-interest to common interest. And it takes courage to lead with moral principles, purpose-driven values and selfless service.

So make the choice to exemplify it all every day. Start by getting everyone committed to your cause, and you will foster an environment in which courage grows. Courage creates candour. Candour enables creativity. Creativity sparks change.

Courage also creates steadiness and the ability to stay the course. When courage is infused in leadership it creates a virtuous cycle that will inevitably get woven into the fabric of the organisation. It is contagious.

Courage creates an environment in which people are able to overcome their natural reluctance to take risks—to take personal risks, to risk relationships or to risk hurting others' feelings. Open the door to courageous conversations founded on trust, unified in purpose.

In order for courage to become truly ingrained, you must be expansive. In an environment where everyone is contributing to outcomes that are valued beyond the individual, everyone expands.

Expansive leaders unleash the leader in everyone. Take a step back, and let the collective shine.

WE'RE NOT IN KANSAS ANYMORE

Our world has been rocked by general purpose technologies over the past couple of hundred years; electricity and binary logic are the big-hitters in this day and age. Binary logic has revolutionised the world in the form of information technology, although a multitude of other uses exist.

We live in times characterised by the digitisation of everything and the disruption of anything. The quantum leaps that await as IT collides with material science and biology now appear boundless.

We live in a second machine age, where business models are fast being redefined by software. The 3D printer is a great example of the potential for binary logic to transform — in ten years' time will we all have one and just self-fabricate? Certainly it has been transformational for the young girl who now has a $2000 prosthetic hand rather than the previous $50 000 option.

With so much change ahead, resistance and fear will be far greater competitors than any disruptor could possibly be.

A culture built on what is best for the customer will encourage everyone involved to embrace the future with excited curiosity, rather than with resistance and fear.

The globalisation groundswell

We all know about globalisation. There are over a billion people online. We are all connected, with more and more of our connectivity being some form of social connection.

If you are sitting at your desk refusing to get 'social' because you think it is a strange world full of narcissism, it is time to rethink.

We live in times when there is a groundswell of collective conscience and community building. Sometimes it goes viral. These communities are created by people who want to connect, who seek meaning, humanity and kindness.

Yes there are people misusing the 'social, connected world' for their personal benefit, who are involved in wrongdoing; but the groundswell underneath is reaching out for positive change.

When this positive change is harnessed, you start to move things. Social technology creates a new mindset where transparency and privacy take on a whole new meaning. Communicating only through traditional methods no longer cuts through to the socially connected: you just won't find them there. Send an email to an 18-year-old and you will know exactly what I mean.

The big issues of the world, some of which have been around for a very long time and some of which are completely new, include climate change, escalating ecosystem destruction, polarisation of societies' wealth, poverty, hunger, and resource scarcity, to name a few.

Meeting these global challenges will require a paradigm shift in leadership: we need the collective, connected leader to emerge.

Step into the collective

Our challenging future requires collective and connected leaders. The best way to describe this sort of leader is to look back in history—you'll find them wherever you find a well-managed crisis.

In every crisis response that I have led or been involved in, it's when the leader has evaluated the situation from a whole-crisis vantage point that they have connected everyone. See the whole system impact—through the eyes of everyone involved, with an open heart, and in collaboration with other organisations.

There is resounding sentiment shared by everyone, which is not divisive—it is connecting. The collective leader is mindful of the cognitive as well as the emotional. They are working with all stakeholders, opening the door to trust—fostering a safe environment for honest, collaborative and collective thinking.

In *Leading from the Emerging Future* Otto Scharmer and Katrin Kaufer describe three 'openings' required for transformation. In opening the mind we challenge our assumptions; in opening the heart we make ourselves vulnerable; and in opening the will we see what is really possible.

The concepts discussed in this section are like an ecosystem: leadership qualities that create a community of people in conjunction with the non-human components of their environment and enable them to interact like a system.

Become the learning leader

In a rapidly changing world our leaders and our organisations need to be learners. Lead learners:

- share willingly and openly; are collegial

- are comfortable with not 'knowing'

- are curious

- think like a young person, regardless of age; are willing to embarrass themselves

- embrace uncertainty

- fill the room with thinkers, the bold; seek out those on the perimeter.

Become the system leader

Welcome to the age of the system leader, where thinking is expansive. These leaders see the whole system. Leaders who operate at a systemic level:

- see the inner and outer connections—from constituents to the environment to the community

- get outside their comfort zones

- build the mindsets of those around them

- are observers and listeners

- engage in open and critical conversation: ask many questions

- see short and long; understand cause and effect; look local and global

- look for links between behaviour and organisational structure; inspect what they expect; run celebration circles

- create the right structure; change and pivot; #flearn

- are intuitive and make intuitive decisions

- test assumptions and ideas; learn; prototype; release the inner child!

- see all perspectives

- consider patterns, trends and unintended outcomes.

'The Dawn of System Leadership' article and webinar from *Stanford Social Innovation Review* is an excellent resource for anyone wanting to know more about system leadership.

Don't be a hero

As much as everyone likes to be the hero, believe in heroes and be buddies with the hero, leaders who want organisations to thrive and succeed, with or without them, need to make sure they are *not* the hero.

The measure of a great leader is the one who walks away and everyone says, 'Look what we have done'. The work of a great leader sustains itself, when they are there and after they are gone.

No egos, only outcomes. Easy to read, hard in practice.

Big, bad biases exist

There is so much to read on the subject of cognitive bias, and so little time. There's everything from 'halo bias' (where that one powerful statement is all you need to hear) to 'unconscious bias' (which clouds your organisation's hiring process) and 'confirmation bias' (which keeps us smoking, drinking and eating—and working too many hours at our desks—until we actually get sick).

In the age of information, cognitive dissonance is only going to become a greater challenge. Take a constant diet of new information mixed with our inner desire for internal consistency, blend in a lot of change, and it gets hard.

No wonder it is so hard to lead. No wonder we have gaps and cracks. No wonder leadership is so topical; the tricky stuff always is.

If leadership was easy I guess there would be more great leaders.

Snapshot: Quick guide (if that's even possible) to leadership

1 Look to the future and embrace 'complications'.

2 Get to know your underberg.

3 Get to know your blind spots.

4 Know who and what you have to *be* to lead with purpose.

5 Collective leadership requires *genuine* connection and community.

6 Get to know your biases.

7 Develop three new leadership foundations routinely—start with courage.

8 Hold on tight and strap in. Great leadership is relentless.

CHAPTER 4

OPERATIONS

B efore starting this chapter I would like to take a moment to define exactly what the O in PLOT represents.

When we think of operations, it is easy to imagine someone with a furrowed brow, a clipboard and probably a few pencils in their top pocket. That is, if you haven't fallen asleep yet—even the word 'operations' is often met with a tired sigh before the first workflow has even been laid down!

So, first things first. Please remove your mental image of the operations manager, the production line and the processing team when you think of operations. 'Operations' is not a job title, and it's not a specific function.

While you're stripping away these outdated notions, also remove the notion of efficiency over effectiveness. Sometimes efficiency isn't preferred over taking a little longer to be effective.

In layman's terms, operations embodies anyone who is doing anything on behalf of your organisation — the activities of any role.

The power to act.

The heart of everything

Operations can be anything from strategy to finance, sales to manufacturing — the list goes on, depending upon the size of your organisation. Independent of roles, structure, culture and governance, *everyone* is doing something. Everyone has the power to act on-purpose.

It is within this all-encompassing context that I will be using the word 'operations'. But before we go further, the important thing to ask is what's directing all of this all-encompassing action.

In the film industry, directors fulfil the vision of the movie. They marry the story's content with its narrative structure and the film's visual design. They are doing the *what* and the *how*.

In the words of film director Martin Scorsese, 'To be a writer, you need a pen. To be a painter, a brush. To be a musician, an instrument. But to be a filmmaker, you need the collaboration of others to bring your vision to the canvas that is the movie screen'.

This is why your clear, shared purpose — supported by a colourful vision with its cast of strategy, values, principles, goals and policies — will be your director.

So, get the 'director' who looks after *what* and *how* and to ensure your purpose is woven through the social fabric of your organisation. Align every single detail of the operations to the organisation's purpose — monitor it and make sure it is on track every step of the way. The 'director' is not a role; it is the all-encompassing plan to embed purpose in everything you do.

By connecting every layer and surface of the operations to a meaningful cause, you will bring out the best in everyone, because everyone is affected and on board. This creates an enabling environment, not only for the organisation's purpose but also for everyone's own higher purposes and aspirations. You only have to go to one yoga class to hear the classic, 'where attention goes, energy flows'. All of a sudden everyone starts to live a purposeful life.

I like this quote from John Eldredge: 'Most of us live in a fog. It's like life is a movie we arrived to 20 minutes late. You know something important seems to be going on. But we can't figure out the story. We don't know what part we're supposed to play or what the plot is.'

It is easy to know the plot when you are part of it—when the director has made it very clear. (And even if you do drop in halfway through the movie, all the actors are on cue, so it is very easy to catch up.)

The flow-on from purpose-rich operations

When you're operating with infused purpose, and the social structure resonates with it, the collective knowledge and experience becomes institutionalised. This gives you a hard-to-replicate, hard-to-tear-apart competitive advantage.

You are weaving a beautiful artisanal meaning through the social fabric of your organisation. As my boss always used to say, 'It's the way we do business around here'.

Customers feel it when they do business with you, not just through your products and services, but also through the attitude and energy of your teams. By creating a culture of serving—serving your customers—religiously promoted by all levels of management, it lifts the moral level of everyone, organisationally and individually.

Does this mean that there aren't bad days? Certainly not. But when you have a strong culture everyone is able to quickly knit things back together if threads start to unravel.

Design the shape for your purpose

The big O in your operations starts with how purpose and strategy are built into your organisational design and structure. Taking a leaf from architecture and industrial design, form follows function, and your organisational 'shape' should be based on the intended purpose and strategy; and it should continue to shape and mould itself as your strategy develops and transforms.

Organisational structures or models come in many shapes and sizes, ranging from traditional top-down hierarchy to geographical divisions, autonomous units and ones that are matrix-managed (to name a just a few). It is important your structure supports what you are trying to achieve.

Whether we like it or not, the way something is designed helps determine how it will behave. You only have to compare the firstborn with the 'baby' of the family to know that for sure!

There are new organisational models in the market that are worth considering, given the pace of change and what we have been discussing in this book. From self-managed to self-organising models there are exciting alternatives for those ready to break ranks, so to speak. Those who are not quite ready to break ranks but who would prefer a purpose-centric approach might like to have a look at Holacracy.

HOLACRACY

Holacracy is a structural alternative that has purpose at its core. If you check out the website holacracy.org and watch the video clips you'll see statements like, 'Holacracy is a social technology for the conscious organisation, one built around core systems and processes which harness the conscious capacity of all within to express the organisation's purpose'. According to its website, Holacracy transforms:

- Culture: Move beyond 'all about the people' to 'all about the purpose'.

- Structure: Get the benefits of an organic structure without artificial hierarchy.

- Decision making: Give everyone a voice, in a rapid, purpose-driven process.

- Discipline: Get deep business discipline without compromising your values.

- Purpose: Help the organisation wake up and pursue its own calling in life.

Zappos, a purpose- and mission-led company with the customer as its core and the agility to move quickly, is currently implementing the Holacracy structure. Now this may not be your cup of tea, but it *is* food for thought. If function follows form we need to make sure our structures reflect our cause and who we want to be. Structures act like symbols in your organisation, whether they work or not—and sometimes their form just speaks for itself. If you want creative thinking, make sure everyone can reach the top.

Money, money, money

Simply stated, money is your fuel, an input variable for fulfilling your purposeful purpose. It is not your outcome. Your outcome is achieving your purpose.

When your operating budget shifts from controlling your organisation to enabling it, focus and attention will be on achieving present-day outcomes through purpose-led behaviour. Profit can then be your future fuel for achieving your purpose.

'Making budget' becomes a celebration of value and standards of excellence, rather than a tick-in-the-box for job security and bonus allocation. Purpose-led leaders build for the overall organisation, not just their profit and loss statement. Perhaps a new hat is required, the 'O'range hat, for operating on-purpose.

This hat takes every operational action, including its budget, and aligns it to its purpose. Perhaps the hat should be purple. I digress.

Systems are no different; they too need to be woven into the purpose. All those management systems, and all that administration that every organisation needs to have in place, are no exception. They should be a reflection of your purpose—an enabler—rather than deflection.

Performance and recognition management systems bring the highest risk of all. Get them wrong and you risk everything, from your brand and reputation, to defeating your purpose.

Knowing your purpose extends beyond the quantified and measurable. Performance management must include intangibles; reward the collaborative, the courageous, and the consistent. If they are not part of the tally that ticks the reward or bonus box they are just platitudes and nice-to-haves. The world is full of grey—design systems that measure it and value it.

Servicing constituents the world over

(Firstly, an aside. I prefer to use the word 'constituents' over 'stakeholders', as it is more collaborative and less hierarchical in tone. However, if you prefer the word 'stakeholders', just mentally replace it every time I write constituents.)

Three to four key constituents often collide within most organisations: customers, employees, community and, for publically listed companies or those about to list, shareholders and/or venture capitalists. When your purpose is not clear and it doesn't relate to your constituents, the people who are trying to get stuff done may get confused.

The classic 'but what about this or that?' (my favourite is 'shareholder value') gets dropped into the decision process like a bomb, particularly when a difficult decision has to be made. Confusion and cynicism creep into the room. The worst part about that behaviour is that it adds no value. It just distracts.

Looking after your constituents is not easy, but somebody has to be centre stage. There must always be a protagonist. Since any organisation worth its purpose-driven salt needs to be outward-facing, your customers are most often going to have to be your protagonists.

Putting shareholders to one side, what about our people — our employees? Surely they cannot simply be a means to our customers' ends? To our own ends?

The answer is well researched, but in my own simple terms: when everyone is working for employees first, you become an inward-facing organisation. Self-interest may sneak in, and customers lose. When purpose and meaning are *operating* in your business (the *what* and *how* you do things), where trust, respect and dignity abound, people become the end in themselves, and for themselves. Operations are directly in line to benefit from this harmonious, focused and autonomous culture working for the same far-reaching purpose.

We have spoken a bit about building communities, such as working in community with our customers. But what about our community's all-important surrounds, inclusive of our beloved mother earth? Sustainability is not some hippy rant or centralised corporate program. It is a reality: it's about stopping to make sure our purpose enhances our community rather than negatively impacts, diminishes or damages.

When our purpose considers the entire community and its surrounds, we have the ability to create intentions and turn them into tangible actions—in addition to corporate social responsibility and charitable foundations. In this way we mesh with our community and mutually benefit one another, rather than cause friction and disconnect.

To lead we must manage

To drill deeper into the management involved in being on-purpose, let's look at how a strong purpose affects the way we manage. Or rather, first let's look at how a blurred purpose affects managers.

Managers operating without a clear purpose can become wayward in many ways. Individualist plans and values sneak in. Unclear measures that are narrow and self-serving may take over; or they end up just managing to the budget, literally. Personal wealth accumulation becomes the measure of success, rather than the creation of value—and it's dangerous when leaders are focused only on their career and its trimmings.

A personally driven purpose can result in many negative outcomes for the organisation and its culture, and it risks becoming authoritarian, bureaucratic and a fairly toxic place to be. The knock-on effect is that performance measures become myopic, as they are serving the wrong purpose. The outcome oppresses rather than enables the human spirit.

In a world where your knowledge worker is your competitive point of difference, this is a risk you cannot afford to take.

As harsh as this all sounds, it is something we must consider.

You can control the process

We have probably all worked for organisations we felt were at odds with our purpose, or not fulfilling their own stated purpose. Or worse yet, lack any clear purpose other than the numbers written on the wall. Before you decide to walk out, consider this.

As a leader (and we all are leaders), you have the choice to bring purpose to the projects you work on. Step up and own the purpose across your projects—whether it is a single event, a specific task or an entire product roll-out. By creating a compelling purpose and applying the PLOT Framework you can build a 'ring fence' around you (and your sanity). You might even want to test it on your personal life!

As a parent or a friend, you can bring your own purpose to the relationships you care about, right up front and centre. Maybe you can't change the world just yet, but you can bring positive change through your own personal purpose-centric projects—both inside and outside of work.

How do you keep good people?

To bring purpose into your ring fence, so to speak, is all well and good, but to really up the ante you need to surround yourself with people who live with purpose, whether you inspire your existing team in this direction or align with different constituents as you work on-purpose. When you find these people, how do you keep them?

Loyalty is a two-way street; it is rarely given when it is not received. But once you have loyalty from your constituents, including your suppliers, you have a competitive point of difference derived from human capital that is impossible to fabricate, no matter what printer you are using!

Organisations are organisms filled with people. They fade or flourish. Loyalty brings motivation, commitment and meaning. Loyalty by its very nature extends beyond your private self, and when linked with a cause—your organisation's cause—you unleash commitment and motivation that extends beyond compensation and position. Just ask anyone who has ever left an organisation why, and the answer will most likely be richer than 'money'.

Loyalty and morale go hand in hand. As Benjamin Morrell once said, 'Morale is when your hands and feet keep on working when your head says it can't be done'.

Creating loyalty in large organisations

The larger the organisation, the harder it is to achieve unity and meaning—let alone a consistent customer experience. When you take all of the departments that are woven into an organisation's structure, it can become overwhelming, stretching out from Human Resources to Marketing, to Risk to Finance, to Legal to Supply Chain Management, to Manufacturing and to the Front Line—and on it goes.

How can large organisations have flexibility, agility and everyone on the same page?

The short answer is: a clear purpose, with a supporting 'director' operating all the *whats* and *hows* of your business. This will enable line managers, divisions, business units, suppliers, separate brands (and so on) to operate as a reflection of the purpose through their area of responsibility.

Specific goals and measures are then set with the common purpose as their nexus, directing all decision-making. You may need to revisit your documentation, systems and communications, but it will be worth it in the end.

From the simplest to the most complex, coherence is achieved through unification under a single purpose. The potential explodes when the meaning and values of your purpose pervade all constituents, no matter how big your organisation.

Lens of rationalisation

No matter where you sit in any organisation, operational decisions and tasks are taking place by the hundreds, every day.

Each transaction, each project, each business plan, each cup of coffee — they all have the potential for a sliding-door moment that could lead either to meaningful purpose or to misguided experience.

Human behaviour has the innate ability to rationalise, to superficially see something as reasonable or valid even when it may not be so. Rationalisations can erode the honesty and integrity of anyone, and any organisation.

Distance from your customers hands you a skewed lens through which to rationalise even more readily. We saw it in the global financial crisis with mortgage-backed securities, where distance from customers was mixed in with incentives and measures to up the ante. Where was their purpose, beyond profit?

There is good and bad in all of us. We are human. So, operationally speaking, if humanity and ethics are part of our organisation's social fabric, and purpose is our daily thread, then the sliding doors should swing right. Without this framework we leave ourselves open to risk.

The enquiry model

When your purpose is viewed through the lens of the customer everyone can start asking relevant how questions. How is this going to impact our customers' price point? How is that going to impact our customers' service experience? 'This' and 'that' are everything, from the complex to the simple; and 'how' becomes a powerful word with purposeful context.

And when you are infused with meaning, you can add in questions like, 'How will this make our customers feel?' and 'How is that going to make our employees feel?'.

When you get to the *how* and you have created trust, you enter a realm of new possibilities. These kinds of questions, this type of honest enquiry, creates possibilities rather than fear.

Here is a framework to open up your organisation to these purposeful, more meaningful questions. Ask:

- How can ... (we do this on-purpose)?

- How can ... (we understand how this feels, is perceived)?

- What could ... (be possible, be the root cause, be different)?

- What can ... (we calibrate, change, improve)?

- What have ... (we learned, tried, explored)?

- What impact ... (could we be causing)?

- What needs changing and disrupting?

When these types of questions become exciting rather than threatening, you know you are on your way. Ditch any egos at the door and knock on purpose.

Purpose-led projects

Being on-purpose reads powerfully on paper but how does it translate to a typical purpose-led project?

To start with, we need to acknowledge that anything we do in business can be managed like a purpose-led project, no matter how seemingly minor.

Traditional project methodology, Agile methodology and simple structures (such as task lists) that help you to get stuff done all share the same basic requirements. Here are the two simple questions that should kick-start every purpose-led project.

1 Why does the project exist?

2 How are we going to deliver on the *why*?

Review the ten most common reasons why projects fail, and you'll see that most of them are directly linked to these two questions. Build them into your projects to help keep you on time, on budget and, most importantly, on-purpose.

In your next project, make sure purpose and vision are defined at the start and are supported by cascading goals and metrics. The possibility of failure decreases substantially, particularly when your answers are directly linked to the overall purpose of your organisation.

This direct link also prevents the ever-so-common multiple disconnects between projects. Purpose-centric organisations tally and view major projects as a total system, built to meet their overall purpose.

Sounds easy, but in large organisations operating with complex technology this is significant, and the stakes are high. Without purpose being the constant through-line, bespoke projects and their silos can dominate your business, creating inefficiencies and inconsistency. This purpose-led approach does not preclude creating 'test and learn' pockets in your organisation, or running high-speed IT teams to be nimble—we dig into this further in chapter 5 (Technology).

Dealing with the devil

The detail. The devil is in the detail. Requirements, design, forecasts and estimates, planning, decisions, small data, big data, configuration, information management, quality, project documentation: it's all part of any project, any goal, and even some simple tasks.

It's one thing for leaders(that's all of us) to work together, but we need the follow-through. A focus on operational detail is vital to realise a purpose and unite everybody through it on a day-to-day, minute-by-minute basis.

How the devil do you get that right in a world that wants to move so quickly? Clearly you need the right people and resources, but what keeps it all together when the going gets tough?

A recent program of work I was involved in was in the area of banking modernisation. It was probably one of the most successful modernisation and transformation programs in the southern hemisphere. The management of the detail was outstanding, but from where I stood it was the leadership at the top and the laser-sharp purpose that made the difference.

Migrating data for financial institutions is serious business, and getting it wrong is not an option. Migrations take out everyone's weekends. What I loved about the migration planning for this particular project was seeing who worked on the weekends. Major migrations had senior executives on site, participating.

At the end of the all-nighter, with a successful migration in the bag, you almost feel a bit superfluous. What did you actually do other than wear your comfortable clothes and show up? Since no decisions had to be made due to a flawless migration, was being on site and awake all night a waste of your time? Couldn't the same outcome have been achieved if all the senior executives had been tucked in bed?

Being on site, in situ with your team, matters. You cannot simulate the visceral. Get in on the ground and you will really know how your business is operating. Get right into your projects and goals; don't just gaze down, allowing the details to become a distant blur.

What we measure matters

Transparency. Rule number one: everything needs to be transparent. The greater the transparency the greater the trust. In any situation we all have the capability to cheat a wee bit, to rationalise, to contextualise — it comes with being human.

This is why transparent measures help mitigate accidental or deliberate bad behaviours. It's also why Enron and Lehman Brothers disturbed and jolted so many people: the auditors, the people we trust to be transparent, broke the cardinal rule. They kept the cloak on; perhaps they read too much Harry Potter.

Take your cloak off and let everyone see the good, the bad and the ugly. Measure success against your purpose, vision, strategy, goals, values and principles. Get your actors and your director out in front. Everything else will follow.

Your financial measures should reflect the value of your organisation, not act as a mirage to obtain stock price growth or investment. Your financial measures are the end state of purpose, vision and strategy.

Measure the voice of your customer loud and clear. Get into the detail. The pearl of every great piece of customer-satisfaction data is not in the top-line rating, it is in the minutiae.

The metrics we use internally to measure our performance will always affect behaviour. It is just human nature. Getting the metrics right is critical to achieving your purpose. Get them wrong and you have an upside-down purpose (your organisational purpose becomes, 'to meet my performance metrics').

I actually find jokes of the 'that's not in my KPIs so I am not going to do that' variety quite unnerving, especially when they're made by leaders. And they're chilling from the point of view of the customer, the environment and the community.

If your business operates through a distribution network, then getting these measures right is also critical. Distribution networks, channels, franchises, brokers — they are all representing your brand — and without a direct link to your purpose it is highly probable that self-interest will prevail.

All parties linked to your organisation — everyone that plays a role in delivering your products and services — should be sharing your purpose. End of story.

At an operations level, sharing performance measures gets everyone linked to a common cause. For example, if excellence in customer service is core to your purpose, why wouldn't you have your suppliers' success measured on *your* customer satisfaction scores?

Build metrics into your supplier contracts that represent your competitive intangibles. When you hear the stories of supply-chain disconnect it is always easy for the person on the outside to see the obvious, hindsight being a very powerful tool. So how do we prevent these disconnects? By connecting the end-to-end delivery chain.

Reporting lines and silos always seem to cause complications, no matter how big or small. Fears of job loss, team size and scope, lost opportunity for experience or education, lack of senior sponsorship and so on can be overcome in a culture that lives for its purpose. So when change hits, our teams and structures need to embrace and invite the change rather than resist and push against it.

Who cares what your job title is, really? Isn't contribution all that really matters? Many companies are starting to eliminate job titles — how comfortable are we with that? I once went from a team size of about 180 people to one of about 14. Everyone asked me if I was upset, did I feel demoted. Not at all. It was simply a new opportunity (which, in truth, has probably been the most transformative of my career to date). A testament to less is more and perhaps size doesn't matter.

Momentum of data

Traditional silos such as business, marketing and IT are now set for a collision course — or a collaboration course, depending on your approach. The way you direct and operate will determine how it plays out in a world where big data and digitisation demand agility, speed and the attitude that failure leads to success.

Suddenly your IT team is either fracturing or bonding with your new high-speed IT team, the one you had to create to get rapid deployment of new technologies without causing downtime. At the same time your marketing department (led by your chief marketing officer, CMO) and your IT department (led by your chief information officer, CIO) are merging paths. Previously the CMO was your brand steward and creative edge, and the CIO was your back-office and infrastructure bedrock. Nowadays they collide with 'the business'.

The business, your front office, needs rapid digitisation at the customer interface and in product development, operational systems and business processes. Worldwide data volumes are growing at a rate of over 40 per cent a year—and you need to agree on and scope the detail to drive these insights. A new way of working is required.

Silos will be organisations' own worst enemy, particularly if they are allowed to continue in the hands of a leader without a meaningful cause and purpose. Technology drives all of this.

Data waits for no-one. Perhaps it's time for a cup of T?

Snapshot: Quick guide (if that's even possible) to operating with purpose

1 'Operations' is a summary term describing how your purpose functions in your organisation.

2 Design for purpose. Form follows function, and your organisational 'shape' should be based on the intended purpose and strategy.

3 Bring everyone with you, and don't forget your supply chain.

4 Start every project *with* purpose and complete every project *on*-purpose.

5 Digitisation and big data impact operating structure. Embrace it! Time waits for no-one.

6 Measure and reward everyone according to the big-purpose picture—keep the director's eye on your vision, strategy and values.

7 Remember that sometimes bad 'ops' can trump even our greatest leaders.

CHAPTER 5
TECHNOLOGY

Technology is revolutionising our world in a way that no-one predicted when those little binary digits popped out all those years ago. This is why it is the fourth and final cornerstone of the PLOT Framework.

Bits of ones and zeroes should connect and create meaning with life, society and our environment for its betterment. When technology is used off-purpose, or worse, used on-purpose for an application without ethics, it has the potential to become anything from a menace to a significant societal danger.

You only have to look to weapons of war to see how a technology's purpose can be bastardised. Corporate technology can easily go astray if not used for a purpose that has a strong moral compass.

Technology has woven and is weaving the planet together, removing the physical barriers that once fragmented the world. There is no better example than the pervasive worldwide spread of mobile phones. Once isolated, now connected; once connected, now interdependent: love it or leave it, this is our economy.

Unprecedented cultural globalisation is shaping our purposes, creating meaning and enhancing relationships—manifesting in what we buy and sell. Our ability to connect is creating a new story, a new model for the human spirit. Who would have thought ten years ago that you would buy shoes from a company who in turn would give a pair to someone, somewhere in the world, who needs them? And that this company would be successful? Who could have imagined that this company's customers would see themselves as a community, connecting and sharing their stories—creating a movement? Thirty-five million pairs of shoes and counting...

...Which circles us back to the first complication discussed in the Leadership chapter. If profit and shareholders are the only ingredients in your purpose, it is very easy to rationalise productivity output levels at a societal level and ignore the devastation to the wider community around it, including mother earth. We see this often, and far too often in developing countries. In this global era, are we using the same measures of success that we would ethically apply to identical work undertaken in our own backyard?

Technology must be our societal enabler. We need to design to stitch together what separates us. Does this mean that every organisation needs a leader to be jumping across the stage chanting 'incubate, accelerate and disrupt'? No. There must always be a balance. We must remember to also be guardians, stewards and trustees. Every organisation needs to find its middle ground with technology.

Technology at work in our modern world is evident not only as a societal enabler but also across learning and education as a whole. This is where curiosity, creativity, problem-solving and critical thinking are fostered, engaging the left and the right sides of our brains simultaneously. This is the glue that brings the artist and the scientist together as technological artisans, to innovate, develop and solve the seemingly intractable while also creating the seemingly impossible.

Get in front of managing your emerging strategy by having innovation as part of the way you do business. Technical artisans can come from anywhere, so let everyone have the opportunity to experiment and spend time in the 'lab'. The lab is everything from mindsets to physical incubators, complex laboratories and your inner venture capitalist. Open the door to innovation and create the opportunity and time to 'go back to school' to foster that divergent thinking that we might have actually managed out of ourselves and others over the years.

Whenever I see the letter T, I cannot help but think of a truss, the kind engineers use to build bridges. Remove it and the bridge falls down. Like it or not, this is why technology is permanently in our PLOT—without it, pretty much every organisation stops. And, just like a truss, the O and the T together form a simple two-force member structure that, when assembled as a whole, behaves as a single object—the *actions* of an on-purpose organisation.

Is your technology telling your story?

The purpose of the T in PLOT is not the actual technology per se, but its application—how we create and manifest our purpose in technology to unlock potential.

There is limitless potential for any technology to serve your purpose in a meaningful way that benefits all constituents. Unlocking your collective human capital's talent for creative application and transformation—rather than remaining mired in silo thinking—connects everyone through purpose. This is the power of technology.

It doesn't matter whether we are talking about nanotechnologies, 3D modelling, biopharmaceuticals, the office intranet or core infrastructure. When you design technology to achieve your purpose you integrate and connect everything, from your human capital to your customers to your suppliers. Interdisciplinary integration from our natural world through to the human psyche transforms organisations and helps break the divide between work and our lives.

With customers at the core of purpose, technology becomes a strategic opportunity to improve the quality of our customers' lives. Understanding and anticipating what customers value, what customers need and what customers may not know they need are all ways that technology executes your purpose. There is nothing more exciting than hearing the whispers of your customers and employees and turning them into a point of differentiation powered by technology.

Technology and your underberg

Technology has this incredible knack of triggering people, particularly when it is broken or perhaps not functioning quite to specification. I believe these triggers run deep under our icebergs and can range from fear of change and fear of failure, to ego and bad past experience.

Imagine the fearful head of manufacturing who has their head in the sand and is not seeking to disrupt their own organisation by looking at 3D printing.

Imagine the fearful head of R&D who is not looking at crowdsourcing design or quantum computing.

Imagine the head of IT infrastructure who is not looking at digital disruption for the front line.

Imagine the organisation that feels social media is for narcissists and refuses to get talking to their customers. (Circle back just five years ago; they were everywhere.)

'Know your customer' is no longer a slogan. If you don't like data analysis, quickly hire someone who does, to mine, farm, forecast and feed your business with customer information. If you like your privacy, best to get out of the front line; customers expect transparency. If you don't really like meeting customers, know that they're coming in through every possible channel, with technology enabling them all the way.

Some people feel uneasy when customers get too close, but technology is going to bring everyone closer, so dig under your berg and embrace being in community with your customers. 'Customer relations' has a whole new meaning, with consumers now 'closing the deal'. Get technology working for you—it is certainly working for your customers.

Try to understand what lies under your organisation that might stop it from progressively adapting to technology. Face the underberg head-on and embrace the change before it takes over and sweeps you or your organisation aside. Be a future-focused leader, using technology as your competitive edge to deliver on your purpose.

Bring the fear of the unknown to the surface and hit it head-on with a culture of curiosity. At the risk of sounding clichéd, disrupt or be disrupted.

The last 10 per cent matters

Technology needs your vision, your knowledge, and your passion to be successful. It also needs plans that get you executing on time and on budget with laser-sharp attention to detail. Technology may be emerging and imperfect in its beta phases, but detail matters at the pointy end. There is no room for complacency.

Technology projects unified in purpose cultivate the environment for establishing rapport, sharing best practice, project alignment and end-to-end compatibility. Most importantly they can foster collaboration founded in shared meaning. Without unification of purpose the potential alternative is technology fragmentation. Incompatibility, multiple customer interfaces, piecemeal infrastructure, and incomplete and unfinished projects. Most significantly, it can create emotional isolation in your organisation. Everyone is probably thinking that this only happens in large organisations, but it doesn't. It happens everywhere. Someone always feels left out, short-changed or redundant—not to mention digitally excluded.

The last 10 per cent seems to be where technology projects go off the rails. It's a bit like a marathon runner with a couple of kilometres to go: you might finish the race but you haven't won it. Something happens—call it a glitch—and the rationalisation lens gets taken out in an effort to keep the project to budget or timeframe. The person looking through the proverbial looking glass rationalises the glitch ('this won't matter', 'this isn't too bad', 'this is kind of to specification')—and you end up with a substandard solution.

Or perhaps you've just lost your competitive point of difference. Or worse, you've actually gone completely off purpose.

Purpose answers the questions of whether, when and how that last 10 per cent matters.

Drilling deeper to put technology into PLOT

Technology is a massive topic, so in this section we'll narrow the focus to three key areas specific to IT: digitisation, transformation and foundations.

Digitisation

Digitisation creates three big opportunities, which in turn demand three big IT essentials, as shown in table 5.1.

Table 5.1: opportunities and IT essentials

Opportunity	Essentials
Connected customers	Executive and business engagement
Big data analytics	Sophisticated systems
Automation everywhere	Seamless performance

The opportunities and essentials in a digital world both have an amplifying impact on your business. Get it right, and you could be cited worldwide as a case study in digital excellence. Get it wrong, and you could be cited worldwide as a case study for all the wrong reasons!

The best thing about getting the essentials right is that when everyone is operating on-purpose you can simply ask two questions:

1 Why would this help our purpose?

2 How would this impact our purpose?

Both simple, but packed with purposeful punch.

With so much opportunity, why isn't everyone diving into digital? Why are those who *have* dived in not often having the time of their lives?

Why aren't large organisations transforming or modernising? Why does infrastructure remain static and then fail because the upgrade patches sit idle on someone's to-do list? How is it that early adopters get left behind?

I think success in IT is a bit like baking a cake. It always looks easy when the cake is set down at the centre of the table — the perfectly risen, perfectly decorated, delightfully moist cake made from scratch. But it's easier said than done.

I may not cook a lot (that's also for another book), but I love baking. And as a baker with IT experience, I share some salient tips in table 5.2.

Table 5.2: baking and the perfect IT project

How to bake the perfect cake	How to bake the perfect IT project
Preheat your oven	Get everyone on-purpose
Find a good recipe and keep ingredients at the right temperature	Find a talented team with attitudes at the right temperature
Measure ingredients carefully	Measure to purpose and celebrate achievements
Use the correct tin size	Plan with agility in scope
Get air into your batter	Give everyone air: foster autonomy and mastery
Cook straightaway: raising agents plus moisture could flop your cake	Implement straightaway: knowledge perishes quickly
Use a good oven and put the cake tin on the right shelf	Create an environment for success and stack achievements on everyone's shelf
Stick to the cooking time indicated	Consider a minimal viable product, or risk competitors rising first

Let's unpack the steps in this table to get your IT rising to success.

1 Get everyone on-purpose

Technology is an enabler. When you keep that front of mind there should be no confusion about how important it is to understand and fulfil your purpose through technology. Technology becomes a core ingredient in your vision and strategy. IT project communications are then centred not on the 'bits and bytes', but on why we are doing this project and how it makes a difference. There are many lessons to be learned from failed IT projects that simply implemented prescribed features rather than creating sculptures for purpose. Constant communication centred on purpose is critical. Repetitive *why* and *how* questions should be celebrated, and the customer should feature in most of them.

Connecting with everyone on a regular basis is critical. Tucking project communications away on your website does not serve your purpose. In start-ups, having only the core team knowing what is going on does not serve your purpose. Communicate accessibly. I like everything on my phone, as do lots of people, so consider a mobile application that enables your purpose—and sharing. I have developed one to help you out; see chapter 6 (Action) for details.

When enabled, technology brings us closer. Imagine your developers in another country sharing photos with your business analysts after they have just successfully reached a milestone—and the business analysts then sharing, and so on. Imagine if every project you ever ran was shared and saved—the intellectual property you'd be storing would be priceless. Imagine the fun you would have sharing the experience across buildings and borders through moving imagery. This is where the technological artisan comes into being. Cross borders and create cultural integration through shared purpose.

2 Find a talented team with attitudes at the right temperature

The need for cross-functional, diverse, skilled and knowledgeable teams is a given. Attitude trumps IQ every time. You need very smart people, but if they are not living the values that underpin your purpose, you will fail. There is little room for ego when team performance is typically going to be your unit of measure.

Grit and tenacity are essential ingredients. Optimism and a sense of humour are mandatory. Everyone's mindset matters (more on this later on, as it's an absolutely critical ingredient). Mindset is your raising agent.

3 Measure to purpose and celebrate achievements

Project and performance measures must be in complete alignment. This alignment needs to flow between the organisation's purpose and the project's outcome. Team members must be measured to these outcomes and they must participate until their requirements have been fulfilled. For example, the business analyst needs to participate in the user acceptance testing. The business representative cannot just show up at the start and finish lines — they need to participate at key points in the program. Senior executives must commit until the bitter end of the project.

Measure what matters. Nourish knowledge by celebrating achievements. Mark your key milestones and take the time and energy to put them on your celebratory shelf. Look after everyone, not just the heroes. Those undertaking consistent incremental work are just as important as the person who cracks the code all night. Senior executives should be tooting the project horn. And never forget the data team — shit in, shit out.

4 Plan with agility in scope

The perfect tin is every baker's dream. Many of us bakers don't have all the tins the recipes say we need, so we need to be agile and flexible but we can't lose sight of the cake we are trying to bake.

Scope is important; knowing what and when changes or pivots are needed is equally important. Clarity of purpose directs decisions, enables new learning to be considered and directs the course of crisis management.

5 Give everyone air

Leaders and program/project managers who create an environment of trust and clear communication enable autonomy. When everyone is operating with agency, the gates to innovation and mastery open.

Track and share decisions transparently. Make governance an opportunity rather than an imposing authority.

6 Implement straightaway

Momentum is critical. Frequently test what you are building—this is critical, too. Be bold and courageous where and when you can; don't be afraid to implement. Tick-tock goes the competitive clock. Right now while you sleep someone in the world is working hard to disrupt your business. So what are you waiting for?

Projects that drag on lose their key people. They get bored. They get recruited. Knowledge perishes quickly. Use it or lose it.

(Don't forget about reporting, because retrofitting it in after you have all your requirements will always leave you short of cash and with a substandard result. Data analytics are now no longer optional.)

7 Create an environment for success

There is a raft of research on the topic of creating the environment for success, from habits to habitats and behaviours to trust and ethics—the forest is thick with trees. So where is the cut-through?

When it comes to IT projects, start with the beneficiary: everyone who is on the receiving side of the project. Keep them front of mind and make sure you have the right people leading who hold them at the heart of the project. Your purpose-driven, ethical, humane leader will get the project over the line, on time and on budget, with the last 10 per cent as your strategic point of difference.

Celebrating success throughout the project is critical. Stack your team's shelves with accolades and thanks each and every day. In most projects, every day matters.

8 Consider a minimal viable product

Minimal viable product (MVP), popularised by Eric Ries (check out *The Lean Startup*), is a great way to start digitising and reduce the risk of your competitors rising first. Does it work for major works, transformation and significant upgrades? My head swings from left to right with trepidation. It depends, but as a method for new ideas and innovation, MVP is fantastic. It is also a great mindset for approaching any IT project.

With all these great ingredients, what's in the way?

The typical answers start with budget, and this is understandable—some projects cost billions. Some projects run over budget by millions, if not billions. So for the sake of this discussion, let's assume there is budget available for digitising, transforming or strengthening foundations.

Everyone from start-ups to government to corporations knows money alone doesn't deliver you an on-time, to-scope IT project. Neither does exceptional talent. The on-time, on-budget, to-scope project has many ingredients; so, looking beyond budget, what can cause it to flop?

I think it lies quietly under the tip of our own icebergs. Thoughts, beliefs, values, traits, motives, self-image, social roles, mindset, structures of influence and relationship, patterns and behaviours—so many variables; surely they are intrinsically linked in the decisions we make about technology?

Fear and ego play heavily into the implementation and adaptation of technology. For the risk-averse, technology presents a world of pain. For those uncomfortable with uncertainty, change is to be avoided. This is where I think humour lands brilliantly. If we can laugh at our fears and get them out into the open, we can then deal them.

As noted earlier, many people have technology triggers. Not least because we perceive technology as something beyond our control in a world that's already pressured—we feel we can't afford to be let down. So let's laugh at these triggers and at our reactions to them.

The great news is that with all of the neuroscience research around, we now know that we can teach old dogs new tricks. So, for all the old dogs out there, fear not—get a digital mentor. It does not matter whether you are the chairman or the start-up in the garage, you need to get digital.

How can anyone run any organisation and not understand the tidal change occurring in the way the world connects and socialises? You can hate social media all you like and lament its narcissism, but there are over a billion people using it. Ignorance is not bliss.

GUIDE TO GETTING OVER THE FEAR OF DIGITAL

FoD? Fear of Digital? The digital-savvy among us are probably wondering what I am talking about. Skip this next section and join us at the other end.

Step 1: Get a digital mentor

Get anyone in an executive position who has FoD a digital mentor. I am a big fan of the student strategy: hire young, bright students. They will brighten up your office and keep you young, and they will be ever so thankful for the experience. Oh, and make sure you treat them as you would any other member of the team, even if they are working fewer hours. They *are* on the team.

Step 2: Use the technology

Start using the technology. Hands-on experience trumps the whiteboard every time. Does this mean you need to be tweeting? No. But you need to know what a tweet is and how people are applying technology for their own purposes—and you need to listen in, because you need to know what people are saying.

If you are in manufacturing, buy a 3D printer and start making something (anything). Tinker, prototype, test, learn—get rid of any fears and just get in there. Under many people's iceberg lies the fear of losing their role to technology. Don't let this be your meltdown.

The Hour of Code (hourofcode.com) is a fantastic online resource used by over 90 million people — calling out the simplicity of writing code. Start with a bit of Javascript, or just jump straight to creating your own Flappy Bird game straight onto your phone. If you're not game to give it a go, just watch the online videos. They feature all sorts, from little kids to the President of the United States — everyone can cut code now! (So why is it that so many of our high schools don't have a computer science course? I think change takes time but I also think there are lots of people with FoD slowing things down.)

Step 3: What to build?

It is easy to be overwhelmed. I have just been looking at a document online illustrating the current providers of marketing solutions, ranging from infrastructure, backbone platforms and middleware to marketing experience and operations. Check it out: cdn.chiefmartec.com/wp-content/uploads/2014/01/marketing_technology_jan2014.pdf.

Imagine if your purpose were hazy? How would you work through that roadmap?

Your digital vision should resonate with your constancy of purpose — you're just using some binary magic to turn it into ones and zeroes. Don't let the mindset of the 'precautionary principle' creep in. You will find solutions for risks, policies and procedures. Develop a mindset of opportunity and abundance, rather than one of misfortune and scarcity.

Consider creating teams that circumvent the current systems and business as usual. You need people on the edges innovating, but like any good IT network design you need both your core and edge devices to get the best performance. Circumvention only works well when you connect and share. Create high-speed IT teams, agile business IT teams, innovation labs led by gurus hired from who knows where — create them all, but connect them back to your people. Don't create a digital elite.

Who's in your community?

Working in community is at the heart and soul of this book: working in community, with the community, with your customers, and with your employees.

Communities are now everywhere. If you don't have one for your customers, you need to create one. Get in community with your customers and you will start to see your purpose come to life, without a single financial transaction taking place. If you do it well, even people who are not your customers will advocate on behalf of your organisation. All you need is a good connection between your head and your heart, some good technology and a customer-focused purpose; your community will do the rest. Build community into your digital strategy. You don't have to look past the experiences of Dell or United Airlines to see what happens when you ignore your customers in a digital world.

Your heart and soul must be in your digital community. You must be authentic. Your authentic selves must be visible in your online communities; otherwise it is just wallpaper. People joining will feel like persona non grata.

Build it as you would your home, welcoming and warm, inclusive for all, founded and designed on-purpose. Everything should symbolise your purpose, values and principles.

Your digital vision should resonate with your constancy of purpose.

Now if you don't care, well don't go digital. There are businesses out there with exit strategies that will see them through without investing in any digital technologies. But if your organisation has a future focus, you must get cracking.

Transformation

Transforming current technology is typically an expensive exercise. You need laser-sharp focus or you could end up wondering why you transformed in the first place. The bigger the budget the more on-purpose you need to be. It is easy to get caught up in the billion-dollar transformation program only to find that you actually could have achieved the same outcome with potentially less money, time or aggravation.

Transformation should be a projection of your purpose. Having leadership that is focused on purpose is critical. When ego steps in you can find your most important program running under someone's iceberg. Everything starts to melt.

Interdependencies between work streams run throughout programs of this size and scale. Traditional silos need to be broken down, cross-functional teams built and extraordinary purpose-driven communication is required.

Grit and tenacity are essential, so everything discussed so far applies. Agility is required, but so are structure and governance—both of which should be celebrated and not denigrated by fast-moving mindsets. Make sure key people in the room remind the over-zealous that although that feature is quirky, it is distinctively off-purpose.

Create a program community and invite all parties, including your customers. The points of intersection will be your blind spots, so make sure you see them up front. Measure every part of the program using the same tape measure you use for your other IT projects. (Otherwise you might mix inches with centimetres. Is that still happening?)

Foundations

While everyone is digitising and transforming, some poor bugger has to keep the business running. Whether your core infrastructure is in-house or outsourced, managing continuity of service and operational uptime is serious business. Holding people accountable is important and when outages occur it is important to dig into them—know what happened and made sure it doesn't happen again. Your celebration circle (see figure 3.1 on p. 145) is what you need—measure performance, reflect, calibrate, integrate and then make sure you celebrate those who are keeping your foundations strong. Losing sight of the people keeping the engine running either has them walking out the door or you are the food source for mediocrity. In my experience it is usually the latter. This is how existing infrastructure falls behind in upgrades; how data centres stay active when they should be heading for the clouds; and how your client data gets dirty. Celebrate the day-to-day. It is just as important to be on-purpose in the present as it is in the future.

* * *

When everyone is operating in unity and is on-purpose, technology becomes your opportunity, not your worst nightmare. The unique position of endless big data (proprietary and open source), intelligent algorithms across digital networks, smart phones which enable their accessibility—now marry all of that with the internet of everything and the digitisation of business processes—and you've got a lot of opportunity.

These technological advancements of the last few decades, along with the monster decade ahead of us, are eliminating labour-cost advantages, along with capital advantages via automation. Computers and possibly large-scale 3D printing are replacing labour, leaving us with our most important advantage—our knowledge—and our IP.

When everyone is operating in unity, technology becomes your opportunity, not your worst nightmare.

Competitive value is critically dependent on how well we manage, skill and lead our people. Knowledge dissipates quickly if left unused, and we need to keep that front of mind. Knowledge needs to be fed and achievement is its favourite food, so celebrate the small stuff as well as the milestones.

Acting for and on-purpose will influence the desire to embrace new technologies, as well as decisions about investment. When they are future-facing and customer-driven, impediments are questioned away.

Snapshot: Quick guide (if that's even possible) to technology

1 Your technology should tell your story.

2 Look at your underberg to find what is slowing you down.

3 The last 10 per cent often matters. Don't let anything get you off-purpose.

4 Making technology projects successful is like getting a cake to rise; mishandled, any of the key ingredients could cause a flop.

5 Curiosity does not kill the cat. It nourishes it.

6 Vision, passion and knowledge plus delivering on time, on budget and to plan is going to get everyone's attention—including those with the cash. (Just have a coffee with any venture capitalist.)

7 Like leadership, success in technology can be exhausting. Strap in and enjoy the ride.

CHAPTER 6
ACTION

The path to being on-purpose is a hard but rewarding one and we hope this book has offered some insights that will help you along the way. This chapter offers resources to assist you to take those insights and put them into action.

Getting everyone on board, *including* your board, requires clear communication and presentation of your purpose. Gauging where you are in relation to where you want to be is important. Plotting your operations and technology — performance to purpose — in relationship to leadership behaviours helps you know what to focus on. Putting purpose in the hands of everyone through their mobile devices increases the likelihood that you will be connecting with your constituents. And finally, nothing beats the face-to-face experience of workshops, speeches and presentations.

My company, BEact, offers several resources to help you get and stay on-purpose. (The company is aptly named as a reminder that we have to *BE* the leader required to *act* on-purpose. I cannot even begin to share how hard it was to secure a relevant company name, so if you don't like it, please don't tell me, because I might have to cut my left ear off...)

Visit www.BEact.com.au to find the resources below. The first three are a gift from me and the fourth is custom-designed.

Presentation templates (PowerPoint and Prezi)—to fast-track getting your PLOT in front of everyone

PLOT Framework—a gauge to keep you on-purpose

BEact mobile application—an app to track and gauge progress, receive tips, log insights and share (customisation and integration available)

Presentations and workshops—keynotes, custom-designed workshops and immersion programs to shape and define your company's PLOT.

A few notes regarding the BEact mobile application: Having your purpose sitting on your phone or tablet will keep you on track—gauge yourself, grab some tips and monitor and measure what keeps you on-purpose and, equally important, off-purpose. The application is to help you turn it on—get everyone you work with using it, including your supply chain. Connect, get sharing and become a collective community. It has been designed to be simple so that you don't think, as we say in my family, 'Now *that's* a job'.

The PLOT Framework

The PLOT Framework (see figure 6.1) functions as a gauge to track your progress towards being on-purpose and to highlight areas for focus and development. The aim is to have everything you do landing in the top right-hand quadrant, manifesting purpose: you, your leaders, your operations and your enabling technology—all through the strength in your clarity of purpose.

Figure 6.1: PLOT Framework

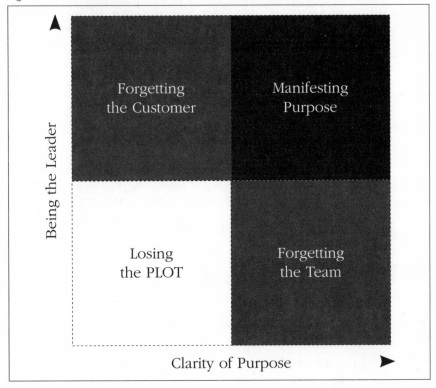

The horizontal axis, Clarity of Purpose, represents our progress in defining, communicating and knowing our purpose. The vertical axis, Being the Leader, represents our progress towards becoming the leader we need to *be* to actualise our purpose. Plotting the progress of your operations and technology indicates whether you are acting and executing on-purpose.

It is probably a good idea to start now, with yourself. Read through the next section and then go back to figure 6.1 and see where you think you fit in. Are you living your life on-purpose? Are your head and heart connected? Are you fragmented or whole? Where does the way you live your life plot within these two axes? Does the use of technology in your life reflect your character and purpose?

After you have plotted yourself, move to your work and use the framework to help get you to a high-performance, on-purpose organisation. You may want to plot this at a divisional level, a geographical level, a managerial level, a project level—whichever suits your particular structure or interest.

Quadrant 1: Losing the PLOT

The lower left-hand quadrant represents the person or team who is, as it says, losing the plot. They are not sure why they are doing what they are doing. They are not sure how they feel about it all. They can't tap into their emotions—they're just operating from the head, staring at the bottom line. This could just be a bad day—but know why that is so that you head out of this quadrant quickly.

Changes are needed and they are probably required at the leadership level. Get the right people on the proverbial bus and define or redefine your compelling purpose, with cause and meaning.

Quadrant 2: Forgetting the Customer

The top left-hand quadrant is the person or team who is starting to connect their head with their heart. They are discovering the power of the connection, but frequently forget the purpose on the journey. They are doing a lot of talking, but it is not translating into the walk that gets them on-purpose.

People like them but may not be sure what they are doing, let alone why they are doing what they are doing. The customer bears the brunt: strong leadership without purpose means the customer may get overlooked. (The employees are happy, but that isn't enough for your customers.) This should be an easy problem to resolve.

Review how purpose is understood, communicated and measured. By celebrating achievements that are on-purpose you will accelerate progress. Incremental as well as disruptive changes should be encouraged. Direct customer feedback creates a high-speed purpose drive. In-situ customer engagement gets everyone to the pointy end—when you can see and feel the impact you are having it changes everything.

Quadrant 3: Forgetting the Team

The lower right-hand quadrant is the person or team who is starting to deliver at about 50 per cent of the purpose, but the execution does not embody the required values and principles. The rubber hits the road for values and principles when you have the difficult conversations with high performers who are delivering 'the number' but not the meaning. Simply stated: is this how we do business around here?

Look for the demonstration of your values and principles through behaviours, symbols and celebrations. Give tangible examples in your crucial conversations.

Achieving outcomes in spite of values and principles may deliver short-term results but they will not sustain your competitive advantage and they will, over time, alter the morale and culture.

Your free thinkers, entrepreneurs and soulful people will leave first. Erosion sets in and before you know it, threads of excellence start to fray and pull apart your organisation.

Quadrant 4: Manifesting Purpose

You have landed in the right quadrant. The top right-hand corner represents the person or team who is starting to manifest purpose. Individual and organisational ends are connecting. Confidence is on the rise. Trust opens the door to constructive conversations. Learning from failure, candour and diverse thinking are all celebrated. Creativity and innovation are a natural, not a prescribed, state of being. Meritocracy has replaced politics. Mastery and autonomy are permeating all levels of the organisation, from the factory to the front line.

Shared purpose keeps everything simple. At the top right you can be sure that everyone is bringing their humanity to work, and that ethics and dignity weave through the fabric of your organisation — making everyone a better person along the way.

Nirvana, perhaps. Possible, I believe.

AFTERWORD

The pace at which we can reach our destination of economic
bliss will be governed by four things — our power to control
population, our determination to avoid wars and civil dissen-
sions, our willingness to entrust to science the direction of
those matters which are properly the concern of science, and
the rate of accumulation as fixed by the margin between our
production and our consumption; of which the last will easily
look after itself, given the first three.

Meanwhile there will be no harm in making mild preparations
for our destiny, in encouraging, and experimenting in, the arts
of life as well as the activities of purpose.

—*John Maynard Keynes, 'Economic Possibilities*
for our Grandchildren' (1930).

With all due respect to Keynes, we live in different times. The
margin between our production and our consumption has not
looked after itself. I believe it is time to flip this quote upside down.
The activities of purpose must now come first.

We need to make sure we are stewards and not disruptors of our
planet. We should be, as the Iroquois people believe, considering
the seven generations ahead of us. We need to be future-focused

and address the biases that are stopping us from solving the intractable issues looming in our future. I believe we can do this. I am an optimist.

I believe in the difference our 'teachers' make.

I believe we should all declare our manifesto.

I believe in purpose.

I believe that you must connect your head and heart and bring your humanity to work everyday.

I believe leaders can come from anywhere and we are the leaders of our lives.

I believe in the youth of today. I believe they can change the world. I hope they are my readers.

So PLOT your own course. Tell your own story. Look back over your shoulder and be proud to say you did it on-purpose.

NOTES

Excerpts and notes don't give justice to the great works which have shaped and sculpted my thinking and career to date, helping to bring *On Purpose* to life. It is the *complete* works of these great people that I want to be celebrated and recognised. I would like to acknowledge and give thanks to:

Jim Collins for his absolute classic *Good to Great*.

Sir Ken Robinson for enlightening us all on the importance of education and more importantly what needs to change.

Brené Brown for bringing humanity to the forefront for us all.

Rick Warren for *The Purpose Driven Life*.

Simon Sinek for his brilliant TED talks and books about making Why the most important word in your life.

Seth Godin for sharing the concept of tribes—making the idea of working in the community something every organisation can embrace.

Richard R. Ellsworth for his outstanding work in the area of purpose and leadership.

The Hunger Project for sharing its innovative, holistic approach, which empowers women and men living in rural villages to become the agents of their own development and make sustainable progress in overcoming hunger and poverty.

McKinsey & Company Australia for their generous heart to bring the work of The Hunger Project to corporations and for their thought leadership and generous newsletters.

Harvard Business Review for their amazing work and ongoing commitment to research.

Stanford Social Innovation Review—every quarterly issue brings new insights leading us to a possible new way of working. I recommend this publication to everyone independent of the sector you are working in.

Levy Economics Institute of Bard College Working Paper Collections on the Global Financial Crisis.

C. Otto Scharmer, author of *Theory U*—amazing work for everyone seeking to let go of old beliefs.

***New Philosopher* magazine**—every edition enlightens and helps keep ego in check and grace in your heart.

Saint James Ethics Centre—a unique centre for applied ethics with excellent publications.

SMARTBOARD

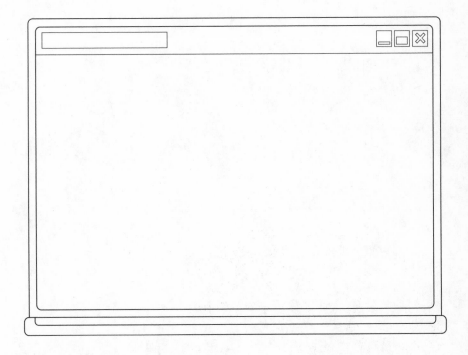

I believe in the Youth of Today.

I believe they can Change the World.

I Hope they are my readers.

 Karen James

INDEX